AS Critical Thinking for OCR
Planning and Delivery Resource File

MR BROCK
RE DEPARTMENT

Heinemann is an imprint of Pearson Education Limited, a company incorporated in England and Wales, having its registered office at Edinburgh Gate, Harlow, Essex, CM20 2JE. Registered company number: 872828

www.heinemann.co.uk

Heinemann is a registered trademark of Pearson Education Ltd

Text © Pearson Education Limited, 2008

First published 2008

12 11 10 09 08
10 9 8 7 6 5 4 3 2 1

British Library Cataloguing in Publication Data is available from the British Library on request.

10-digit ISBN: 0 435235932
13-digit ISBN: 978 0 435467 09 8

Copyright notice

All rights reserved. No part of this publication may be reproduced in any form or by any means (including photocopying or storing it in any medium by electronic means and whether or not transiently or incidentally to some other use of this publication) without the written permission of the copyright owner, except in accordance with the provisions of the Copyright, Designs and Patents Act 1988 or under the terms of a licence issued by the Copyright Licensing Agency, Saffron House, 6–10 Kirby Street, London EC1N 8TS (www.cla.co.uk). Applications for the copyright owner's written permission should be addressed to the publisher.

Typeset by TechSet, Tyne & Wear
Cover photo: M.C. Escher's 'Symmetry Drawing E69' © 2007 The M.C. Escher Company-Holland. All rights reserved. www.mcescher.com
Printed in the UK by Ashford Colour Press

Acknowledgements

The authors and publisher would like to thank the following individuals and organisations for permission to reproduce materials:

Page 25 Extracts from 'Pupils burn blazers in protest at a new rule enforcing uniform' by Simon de Bruxelles, *The Times*, 3 October, 2007, reprinted with permission of NI Syndication. Page 25 Extract from 'Today there are nearly as many interpretations of dreams...' from *Psychologies*, November 2007, p. 80, reprinted with permission of *Psychologies*. Page 26 Extract from 'Common belief holds that women talk more than men...' from *Psychologies*, November 2007, pp. 90–93, reprinted with permission of *Psychologies*. Page 26 Extract from 'More and more singles want help finding a partner...' from *Psychologies*, November 2007, p. 101, reprinted with permission of *Psychologies*. Page 27 Extract from 'Shoppers dive for cover as chef's eye-watering chilli sauce causes a terror alert' by Steve Bird, *The Times*, 3 October, 2007, reprinted with permission of NI Syndication. Page 31 Article 'There are some things that it is unwise to put in your microwave...', from *BBC Focus Magazine*, October 2007, pp. 52–53, reprinted with permission. Page 34 Article 'Our high-street habit is not going away' by Jess Cartner-Morley, *Marie Claire*, November 2007, reprinted with permission of *Marie Claire*/IPC Syndication. Page 43 Extracts from 'More than a quarter of Britons identified with the Royle Family according to a survey' from *The Independent*, 1 October 2007, reprinted with permission of *The Independent*. Page 43 Extract from 'Psychology professor Laura King found that students...' from *Psychologies*, October 2007, reprinted with permission of *Psychologies*. Page 44 Extracts from 'Plastics chemical is harmful, say experts' from *New Scientist*, 11 August, 2007, reprinted with permission. Page 51 Article 'Modern mothers warm to home cooking', *The Times*, 1 October, 2007, reprinted with permission of NI Syndication. Page 51 Extracts from 'Oliver's campaign fails as pupils give up school dinners', *The Independent*, 3 October, 2007, reprinted with permission of *The Independent*. Page 53 Adapted from 'In 20% of sighting a back or body...', www.nessie.co.uk. Page 53 Extract from an article by Magnus Linklater, *The Times*, 3 October, 2007, reprinted with permission of NI Syndication. Page 54 Professor Plume extract and sketch of Loch Ness monster from Nessie on the Net, www.lochness.co.uk, reprinted with permission. Page 55 Picture of the alleged Loch Ness monster, reprinted with permission of Fortean Picture Library. Page 55 Cartoon, reprinted with permission of cartoonstock.com. Page 56 Article, 'Stand up for the Wet Noodles' by Philip Lieberman from *New Scientist*, 3 October 2007, reprinted with permission. Page 93 Extract 'Nokia recently let journalists at its Research and Development centre...' from *New Scientist*, Feedback, p. 92, 17 November 2007, reprinted with permission. Page 93 Extract 'Sociologist think that isolation worsens an area's economic...' from *New Scientist*, 3 November 2007, p. 8, reprinted with permission. Page 94 Extract 'Many people ask whether it is worth trying to cut our carbon emissions...' from *New Scientist*, 17 November 2007, pp. 34–41, reprinted with permission.

Every effort has been made to contact copyright holders of material reproduced in this book. Any omissions will be rectified in subsequent printings if notice is given to the publishers.

Websites

The websites used in this book were correct and up-to-date at the time of publication. It is essential for tutors to preview each website before using it in class so as to ensure that the URL is still accurate, relevant and appropriate. We suggest that tutors bookmark useful websites and consider enabling students to access them through the school/college intranet.

Contents

Introduction ... iv
Lesson Planning ... v

Unit 1 Introduction to Critical Thinking

Section 1 The Language of Reasoning

Chapter 1	Recognising arguments, conclusions and reasons	1
	Worksheet 1.1 Foundation	7
	Worksheet 1.2 Core	8
	Worksheet 1.3 Extension	10
	Worksheet 1.4 Extension	11
	Worksheet 1.5 Extension	12
Chapter 2	Counter-assertions, counter-arguments, hypothetical reasoning and assumptions	13
	Worksheet 2.1 Foundation	17
	Worksheet 2.2 Core	18
	Worksheet 2.3 Extension	19
	Worksheet 2.4 Foundation	20
	Worksheet 2.5 Core	21
Chapter 3	Identifying evidence and examples	22
	Worksheet 3.1 Foundation	25
	Worksheet 3.2 Core	26
	Worksheet 3.3 Core	27
Chapter 4	Analysing and evaluating reasoning	28
	Worksheet 4.1 Core	31
	Worksheet 4.2 Core	32
	Worksheet 4.3 Core	34

Section 2 Credibility

Chapter 5	The credibility criteria	37
	Worksheet 5.1 Foundation	42
	Worksheet 5.2 Core	43
	Worksheet 5.3 Extension	44
Chapter 6	Assessing credibility of individuals, organisations and documents	45
	Worksheet 6.1 Core	51
	Worksheet 6.2 Core	53
	Worksheet 6.3 Extension	56
Unit 1	Guidance to the Activities	58

Unit 2 Assessing and Developing Arguments

Section 3 Analysis of Argument

Chapter 7	Identifying argument components	79
	Worksheet 7.1 Multiple Choice	84
	Worksheet 7.2 Activity	85
	Worksheet 7.3 Activity	86
Chapter 8	Applying and extending analytical skills	87
	Worksheet 8.1 Key terms: Core	90
	Worksheet 8.2 Activity: Role play	94
	Worksheet 8.3 Core	95

Section 4 Evaluating Argument

Chapter 9	Evaluating reasoning: the use of evidence, examples and explanation	97
	Worksheet 9.1 Foundation: Core	100
	Worksheet 9.2 Longer text: Core	101
Chapter 10	Evaluating reasoning: appeals	103
	Worksheet 10.1 Foundation	105
Chapter 11	Evaluating reasoning: flaws	107
	Worksheet 11.1 Core	110
	Worksheet 11.2 Extension	113
Chapter 12	Evaluating reasoning: analogies, hypothetical reasoning and principles	114
	Worksheet 12.1 Extension	117

Section 5 Developing your own Argument

Chapter 13	Basic reasoning skills	120
	Worksheet 13.1 Foundation	122
	Worksheet 13.2 Core	123
Chapter 14	Writing an argument	124
	Worksheet 14.1 Foundation	127
	Worksheet 14.2 Core	128
Chapter 15	Developing your argument	129
	Worksheet 15.1 Extension	132
Unit 2	Guidance to the Activities	133

Introduction

This Teacher Resource File has been written to work alongside AS Level Critical Thinking for OCR, but it could also be used independently of the textbook. Each chapter has the same key features:

- Teacher Notes
  - Discussion of the issues under consideration
  - Learning objectives
  - Common problems
  - Strategies
  - Suggested activities
  - Guidance to the worksheets
- Worksheets

The Teacher Resource File also comes with:

- a CD-ROM and
- Guidance to the Activities in the Student Book.

Teacher Notes

The Teacher Notes are intended to help both the experienced teacher of Critical Thinking and the teacher who is delivering the course for the first time. They are not a blow-by-blow account of what to teach and when, but a set of notes, tips, suggestions and worksheets that should help teachers to develop the confidence and skills to plan lessons and answer students' questions.

The Teacher Notes offer a little background on some of the skills taught and tested and on the rationale for including these skills in the hope that this will help teachers to gain the sort of context they take for granted in their main subjects. They are written from the perspective of an experienced teacher and examiner and try to find a middle path between teaching thinking skills that are useful for life but which do not help students to pass the OCR exam, and focussing too strictly on the requirements of the exam.

Common Problems

In each chapter there are brief notes about common problems that trouble students, both in the classroom as part of the learning process and in the exam as part of the testing process.

Strategies

Strategies are suggested for dealing with the common problems. These take the form of general suggestions and specific recommendations. They are often incorporated into the activities suggested for whole class, group or individual work.

Suggested Activities

In each chapter activities are suggested which should help students to master the skills, overcome the common problems and relate the skills to their lives and other academic subjects. The activities are divided into whole class, group work and individual work, and include media activities, interactive and kinaesthetic activities as well as teacher-led questions and answers, and students working from worksheets.

In some cases, an indication is given of a progression of tasks, which could be done in one lesson or across several teaching sessions. Indications of time taken for an activity are not given, as teachers have varying lengths of time available and groups of varying size and nature. Most activities will take different lengths of time depending on the group, and teachers can allocate time appropriately.

Lesson planning

Lesson planning is a necessary thinking process. It is important to consider the following questions, even if you don't write the answers down:

- What is the starting point for my students (what can they already do)?
- What should they have gained/which skills should they have practised by the end of this lesson?
- What teaching methods will best enable this learning to happen?
- How can I make sure that each student develops their skills (how should I differentiate)?

What counts as a good Critical Thinking lesson?

Good Critical Thinking lessons are varied and variable. That is, they should contain lots of different activities, and each lesson may be very different. There is no single template or formula for a good lesson. Some lessons, such as feedback after exam practice, will be strongly teacher-led. Others will put most emphasis on students working in pairs or groups, or even on students leading class activities. You will develop a feel for what counts as a good Critical Thinking lesson.

Critical Thinking is a discipline that encourages the development of thinking skills. In this respect planning lessons may have more in common with lessons such as music, PE, languages or maths, all of which are dominated by the development of skills, rather than subjects such as history, biology or English literature, which are content-heavy. So it would probably be worth looking at lesson plans from a subject such as music to learn how teachers cope with the development of skills and the different starting points of students.

The three most important aspects of a Critical Thinking lesson are:

- modelling
- practice
- feedback.

These will occur throughout each section of the lesson and throughout the course, and not necessarily in discrete chunks of the lesson.

You will need to model and explain the thinking skill under consideration. This can be done with pre-prepared examples, but also through interaction with students and use of the arguments they produce. You can model the skills in different ways to different students to ensure that they move on from their starting point. So, for example, if Student A struggles, you might model an argument that has one reason to support a conclusion. For Student B you might model an argument that has two reasons, an intermediate conclusion and an example to support the conclusion.

Practice can mean written exercises or interactive games, or group work. Thinking is not visible, so not every practice session will result in written work. The teacher notes and worksheets give a variety of suggestions and activities for student practice.

Feedback should occur during and after practice. It might mean a nudge in the right direction, such as a reminder that we evaluate flaws by showing why this reasoning does not support this conclusion. It might mean a question to make a student think in a new direction. It might mean sharing answers and asking why. It might mean a detailed written critique of students' performance. It might mean peer marking. But it should always include more modelling of the performance that students are aiming at.

Time

Many of the suggested activities in the teacher notes can be stretched or shrunk to fit the length of time you have available. The 'right' length of time will depend on your students.

OCR AS Critical Thinking — Lesson planning

Sample lesson plan

Objectives:
- Revise flaws.
  - All students should know the names of the main flaws in the specification.
  - All students should be able to name key flaws when they come across them in a passage of reasoning.
  - Most students should be able to describe what is wrong with flawed reasoning in general, with some reference to a specific passage of reasoning.
  - Some students should be able to clearly explain why a specific flawed argument does not support its conclusion.

Time: 1 hour 15 minutes
Students: 25
Ability: mixed

Time	Method, resources, differentiation
5 mins	Recap of existing knowledge: Individually, students should write down the names of as many flaws as they remember in two minutes. (Teacher takes register) (Practice) Students work with a partner for 2 minutes to add to list of flaws (similar ability pairs to facilitate later exercise). (Practice) Elicit as many flaws as possible and show complete list on projector (Feedback).
10 mins	Give each pair the names of three flaws using cards produced by photocopying parts of Worksheet 11.1. The pair should define the flaw and explain what is wrong with this reasoning. Differentiate by giving more able students more challenging flaws such as straw person, and give weaker students flaws such as generalisation or attacking the arguer. Target flaws to students. (Practice) Walk around asking questions such as: 'Is that quite right?' 'Have you got the right flaw? Aren't you describing circular argument not confusing necessary and sufficient conditions?' 'Well done, that's almost right, but wouldn't you say extreme and illogical links in the reasoning?' (Feedback and modelling).
10 mins max	Elicit the definitions very quickly (they should be familiar by now), correcting and adding to them where necessary verbally, and referring students to the written list they keep in their well-organised folders/CD with textbook/definitions on the wall of the classroom (Feedback and modelling).
5 mins max	Bingo. Class write names of six flaws. Teacher reads definitions/examples of flawed reasoning (using Worksheet 11.1). Class tick off names when definition or example is read out (Modelling and practice).
15 mins	Dominoes (using Worksheet 11.1). Students match the examples of flawed reasoning to the names of flaws in five groups of five mixed ability students (Practice). Teacher walks around asking questions and pointing out which links are correct and which are not, and encouraging every student to join in, using focussed questions such as, 'Jayne, what do you think is wrong with this reasoning? Can you find the label? Oh, Amir and Sal have used it? Do you think they're right? Why not ask them?' (Feedback).
5–10 mins	When a group has finished, teacher confirms or suggests improvements. Give each student in that group a piece of flawed reasoning from the dominoes game (so they already know the name of it). Ask students to write an exam-style answer, which names the flaw and explains what is wrong with the reasoning, with reference to why these reasons do not support this conclusion. Differentiation by choice of flawed reasoning (really weak students might be given the flaw they worked on earlier) and by outcome – most able will produce strong answers, weaker students will produce definitions without reference to the specific argument (Feedback and model improved performance).
20 mins	Exam practice in timed, silent conditions. Two multi-choice questions re: flaws and longer text with flaws questions. Feedback by peer marking or teacher marking. Provide mark schemes and share strong answers to model good performance. Consider sharing C grade performance with E grade candidates to model something they can aim at.

Unit 1 Introduction to Critical Thinking
Section 1 The Language of Reasoning

Chapter 1	Recognising arguments, conclusions and reasons	1
	Worksheet 1.1 Foundation	7
	Worksheet 1.2 Core	8
	Worksheet 1.3 Extension	10
	Worksheet 1.4 Extension	11
	Worksheet 1.5 Extension	12
Chapter 2	Counter-assertions, counter arguments, hypothetical reasoning and assumptions	13
	Worksheet 2.1 Foundation	17
	Worksheet 2.2 Core	18
	Worksheet 2.3 Extension	19
	Worksheet 2.4 Foundation	20
	Worksheet 2.5 Core	21
Chapter 3	Identifying evidence and examples	22
	Worksheet 3.1 Foundation	25
	Worksheet 3.2 Core	26
	Worksheet 3.3 Core	27
Chapter 4	Analysing and evaluating reasoning	28
	Worksheet 4.1 Core	31
	Worksheet 4.2 Core	32
	Worksheet 4.3 Core	34

1 Recognising arguments, conclusions and reasons

CHAPTER OVERVIEW

Students will be introduced to the basics of Critical Thinking. They will learn to distinguish reasoned argument from other kinds of writing, and to identify its basic components, reasons and conclusions. They will start to work with the precision and accuracy that is important in Critical Thinking.

Why argument?

There are many ways of thinking – for example, reflecting, calculating, imagining, feeling, associating, deciding. Critical Thinking is concerned with the principles that can be used to structure thoughts and ideas. It is characteristic of good, or useful, thinking that it has a structure. Art, music, literature, business plans, mathematical proofs and scientific demonstrations need an organising principle – a structure – in order to be effective. Critical Thinking encourages students to use a rational framework to understand others' thinking and give purpose to their own.

The structure used in Critical Thinking is argument. Argument is reasoned persuasion and needs to be differentiated from emotional persuasion, factual explanation, account or unfounded opinion. This kind of rational organisation of thoughts is useful in most academic subjects and in daily life. The focus on reasoned argument does not mean that other kinds of thinking are not valued. Many of them are necessary in argument. However, we are teaching and testing the use of argument, so we concentrate on students' ability to understand and use the structures of argument.

Simple argument analysis

Student Book Chapter 1 pages 6–15
Specification 3.1.1 1, 2, 3, 4, 5

Assessment Objective (AO) 1 in Critical Thinking is 'Analyse argument.' Analyse here means to break an argument into its component parts and label them. It involves understanding how the components are put together to make the whole.

Students first need to be able to identify an argument – that is, a text that offers reasons to persuade an audience to accept a conclusion. Reasons must give logical or rational support to the conclusion.

Identifying the conclusion within an argument is arguably one of the most important skills that we can help students develop. They are bombarded with adverts, newspaper and magazine articles, radio and TV opinion shows, not to mention everything available on the Internet. If we can help them to identify what they are being persuaded of (or to do) with precision, then they will be better equipped for modern life.

Almost equally important is the skill of identifying reasons. 'On what grounds am I being persuaded to spend my money on this object/go to a certain college/give my support to Dave in the SU elections?' Are these actually reasons to accept this conclusion?

This kind of analysis is probably very different from anything students have done before. It may be very different from anything you have taught before, because analysing argument is all about the connection between ideas rather than the ideas themselves or the knowledge in them. Fortunately, in Critical Thinking, it doesn't matter if you are unsure of yourself. You do not have to be the fount of all knowledge to pass the exam. Asking questions is probably more useful to your students than giving answers. It is really helpful to create an environment in which there is no one right answer. Then students won't be afraid of being wrong, so should be more confident about working through the thinking processes, which are the important part of Critical

Thinking. When it comes to the exam, of course, there are times when there *is* a right answer. If a candidate identifies a reason but calls it a conclusion, they will be wrong. In class, though, it can be more useful to respond with a question: 'Do you think that gives us a reason to accept X? Can you explain why?' Essentially, even in the exam, what we are really testing is the thinking process used to reach an answer. So it is this process that students need to practise in class.

Learning objectives

- Understand the meaning of the key terms: argument, conclusion and reason.
- Identify simple arguments.
- Identify reasons and conclusions in simple arguments.
- Identify and use argument indicators.
- Understand that accuracy is important in Critical Thinking.

Common problems

Some students find it difficult to shake off their prior understanding of words such as 'argument'. They may persistently believe that an argument is a two-sided disagreement. Others may confuse an argument with a discursive essay and be reluctant to move away from the idea that it should have two equal, balanced sides.

Some students understand the concept of argument very quickly and want to move on to more interesting challenges, before they have truly internalised the new concept and skills.

Students generally want to paraphrase reasons and conclusions rather than quoting them precisely. Some students will confuse 'reasoned, objective argument' with 'certain proof'.

Strategies

The key to the first two problems is practice and repetition. You might find one of the following analogies helpful when explaining to students the need for repetition.

When you are learning to drive, you understand pretty quickly that you are aiming to get the car in that parking space without crashing into anything else, hitting the kerb, stalling or making yourself look silly. But even after you've understood that, you have to keep practising until you can do it reliably. Thinking is a bit like that; it's a skill that needs to be practised. Likewise, kicking a ball into a net, turning a somersault, playing the guitar. Equally, it is worth emphasising that, just because a student struggles with a skill the first time, this doesn't mean that practice won't help. None of us is ever likely to be David Beckham, but we could all improve our aim if we practised every day. The same is true of thinking.

Explain to students as early as possible that, when identifying a component of the author's argument, they need to quote it precisely. What we are teaching and testing in AO 1 is the student's ability to identify different components in the author's argument. It's like identifying the carburettor in a car engine. You would expect a student to point at it, not to go away and make something a bit like it.

Where students have too rigid an understanding of 'objective' or 'argument', you will need to explain that Critical Thinking deals with everyday reasoning and that many of the most interesting things cannot be proven. Contrast the following.

A Trees have leaves. Oaks are trees. So oaks have leaves.

B Music helps people to learn by stimulating the brain. It can also help to create calm, relaxing ambience, which puts students in the mood for learning. So it is worth using music in the classroom.

It is much more worthwhile to persuade someone that it is worth using music in the classroom than that oaks have leaves. It cannot be 'proven' in a strict sense, but it can be rationally supported. It can also be rationally countered. Worksheet 1.4 should help this type of candidate think around some of the different kinds of claim and the different standards of reasoning required to support them.

In the activities that follow here, it is occasionally suggested that you give points to students. If you are organised enough, having an ongoing competition, perhaps between teams rather than individuals, with a

1 Recognising arguments, conclusions and reasons

running tally on the board can motivate students. The analytic skills in the first couple of weeks can seem dry, and are a bit of a shock to students who wanted the opportunity to express their opinions and just 'discuss things'. Competitive and group activities can alleviate this somewhat.

Suggested activities

Whole class work

'Football is pointless.' Write this, or a similar statement on the board/screen. Ask students to move to one side of the room if they agree and to the other if they disagree. Either choose two confident, outgoing students or put the whole class into disagreeing pairs. Ask them to role-play an argument or slanging match about this. Allow them to hurl some inventive (non-offensive) insults, possibly provided by you (little books of Shakespearean insults provide some wonderful material in this respect, and are also useful later when we come to ad hominem).

Put students back to their opposing sides of the room. Highlight that they have just had an 'argument' in the everyday sense of the word, synonymous with 'quarrel', 'slanging-match' or 'row'. Say that in Critical Thinking we have a different, calmer understanding of 'argument'.

Elicit why students hold their opinion. You may wish to give a point to any student (or their team) who comes up with a reason (rather than an expression of opinion) why football is, or is not, pointless. 'It does have a point. The point is to have fun.' This would be worth one point. By contrast, 'Football's brilliant', or, 'Football's boring' would not support the claim and would not get any points. Keep asking, 'Why?' When students do provide reasons, you will have the material for one or two short, reasoned arguments. Highlight that the passages on the board are now arguments in the Critical Thinking sense. Delete one of them, and check that students still understand that the one-sided justification of an opinion (now a conclusion) is still an argument.

Other claims you could usefully get students to support at this stage might include: 'Mum, you should lend me the car tonight.' (Make sure students really do focus on reasons that would persuade Mum – rationally, not emotionally – to lend her child the car.) 'You should let me go to Download/on holiday with my friends.' 'College should have a snooker table.'

Lesson starters

At the beginning of every lesson, get students to write a definition of a key term. Alternatively, give them a definition and ask them to write the word, or play bingo with a number of key terms.

Group work

Divide your class into groups. While one group completes a worksheet, give each student in a group of about twelve a piece of paper that says, argument, reason, explanation or conclusion. Spread twelve definitions of these words around the room. Only one definition is correct for each word. Students have to race to collect the correct definition. Those who pick up the correct definition gain one point. Those who are empty-handed gain nil. Those who have the wrong definition lose a point. Worksheet 4.2 supplements this activity.

Individual extension work

Ask students to produce arguments relating to the claims in the worksheets or to claims they have thought of. The Student Book does not cover AO 3, 'Developing your own argument' until Section 5. However, students do not follow a linear progression in the same way that a textbook does. They benefit from starting to develop their own reasoning from the very beginning of the course. This helps their understanding of the logical link between reasons and conclusions.

Photocopy letters pages from a variety of newspapers. Students identify whether each letter is an argument, account, explanation or unfounded opinion. Where an argument is identified, reasons and conclusions can also be identified. This exercise is particularly useful for keeping more able students engaged while you reinforce the new concepts.

Discuss the ideas in the letters and push students to think for themselves about these ideas. They can find it very liberating that their own ideas are valued, and more able students find that this gives them something to think about.

Guidance to worksheet activities

1.1 Foundation

Students are required only to state 'argument' or 'not argument' in their answers. The guidance that follows indicates how these passages might best be described. This should be regarded as a teaching aid rather than a requirement for candidates.

1. a) is random sentences – at most, the third sentence explains why it was possible to have mud fights in summer. b) Explanation. c) Unconnected sentences. d) Argument (Conclusion: It is a really good idea to do something creative). e) Unconnected sentences.

2. a) Because. b) Therefore. c) Because. d) Because. Therefore.

1.2 Core

Students are required only to state 'argument' or 'not argument' in their answers. The guidance that follows indicates how these passages might best be described. This should be regarded as a teaching aid rather than a requirement for candidates.

Before asking students to do task 3 remind them of the discussion you had about what it means for a reason to support a conclusion.

1. a) Information. b) Unconnected sentences. c) Account. d) Argument.

2. Context: We hear so much about yobs.

   R: Most young people work hard, contribute to society, volunteer for charity, and are kind, giving and loving.

   R: They deserve to have their achievements praised.

   C: It would be good to hear more about the achievements of young people on the news.

3. The reasons that best support the conclusions are:

   1 D + I   2 J   3 F   4 O + P   5 A + K

This exercise ought to lead to some discussion about what it means for a reason to support a conclusion. You may find the following comments helpful.

1. D + I: Both of these reasons are necessary to justify the swap from Sociology to History. D gives a reason only to take up History, and I gives a reason only to give up Sociology. Together, they support the whole claim.

   H: On its own, H, 'My Sociology teacher was horrible to me', is not a good reason to support the conclusion that I should switch to History AS from Sociology. It isn't even a good reason to give up Sociology if you enjoy Sociology, and it was only once. This is especially the case as 'being horrible' can often include requiring homework to be handed in on time or objecting to irrelevant chatter. (It might be worth discussing what 'horrible' means in this context, and how horrible and how often a teacher would have to be for this to be sufficient reason for a student to give up a subject.) Together with D and I, H might provide an emotional explanation why someone did give up Sociology for History. But it does not provide rational support for the conclusion.

2. J: If the new colour has an adverse effect on a significant number of students, that would be a reason for the college not to have chosen it. E and G apply only to single individuals, so it would be difficult to use them to justify a conclusion about what the college should or shouldn't have done. E is perspective dependent; if you are the teacher, E will be a reason for you to wish the college hadn't painted the walls orange (although that is still not a reason why the college shouldn't have done it). If you are a student who hates the teacher, E might be a reason to be glad that the walls are now orange. G is a reason why I might wish that the college hadn't painted the walls orange – but that is not a reason why the college shouldn't have done it. From their perspective, orange walls that give one person a headache might be very much better than peeling grey walls which make everyone gloomy and put students off attending college at all.

3. F: Social secretaries organise parties and other social events. If Dave has a track record of organising fantastic parties, then he probably has the organisational skills and imagination to organise good social events for the college. This would be a reason to vote for him. B does not give

us a rational reason to vote for Dave. People are often swayed by such factors, but generally not on a rational level. If ugly Josh would organise better social events than gorgeous Dave, then reason suggests that you should vote for Josh.

4. O + P: This question does rely on knowledge that an iPhone is a mobile phone with an iPod and that it is expensive. Having neither an MP3 player nor a phone, and having plenty of money, would provide some support for the conclusion that 'I should buy an Apple iPhone'. This would be fairly easy to counter, though. It's still only weak support.

C: Having flushed your iPod down the loo would at most be a reason to buy a new iPod – or possibly to manage without one until you can be more careful with your belongings. Something being the latest gadget (M) does not provide rational support for the conclusion that I should buy it. At most it provides emotive support to keep up with other consumers. But if you don't need one, if it doesn't have the functions you want, if it's overpriced or doesn't work very well, then it being the latest gadget does not give you a reason to buy it.

5. A + K: A provides a reason to study media technology and K provides a good reason not to become a plumber. So both are needed.

L: Does not provide a good reason to study Media Technology, as Media Technology leads to careers behind the scenes rather than in front of the cameras. If students have put L, this would support the conclusion that they really need to do some careers and qualifications research!

1.3 Extension

Students are required only to state 'argument' or 'not argument'. The guidance should be regarded as a teaching aid not as a requirement for candidates.

1. a) Not argument. b) Not argument.
   c) Not argument. d) Argument.
   e) Not argument. f) Not argument.

2. R: Businesses want people who are technically competent and can also work in a team (d).

R: They are especially keen to recruit graduates who can explain complex systems in terms that clients can understand (d).

C: New IT and Computing Science courses ought to include business management and communication skills courses (d).

1.4 Extension

Again students are required only to identify which passages are arguments. Other information is for guidance only.

The point of this worksheet is to introduce students to some interesting ideas while reinforcing their ability to identify arguments. It diverges somewhat from the topics that might be found in the Critical Thinking exam. Nevertheless, it should prepare them for work on the nature of claims, and provoke thought about what can and cannot be supported by reasoned argument. This provides a useful opportunity for class discussion and stimulating research which will encourage students to think.

a) Argument.

R: Colour is something that we see, not something that is there in the object.

R: If no one is looking, there is no one to see any whiteness in:

Ex: for example, snow.

IC: So there is no whiteness.

C: Snow is not white.

Students do not need to be able to identify an intermediate conclusion until Unit 2. However, more able students should be able to understand the concept sooner and may need to work with more complex arguments to keep them challenged.

b) Not argument. This tells you why I'm going for a cup of tea. I'm not persuading you to agree.

c) Argument. It's not a very good argument. Students may have some fun imitating it, or taking the ideas apart. But it is important to realise that even weak arguments are arguments.

R: It is only snow because we say it is snow.

IC: Snow doesn't exist independently of us.

C: So snow is not snow.

d) Not an argument. It doesn't make sense to express this concept as an argument. It may be worth introducing and discussing the concepts of maths, of mathematical truth, of how we know that $2 + 2 = 4$, of whether we are certain about this.

e) Redefinition of a circle.

f) Argument. This is an example of a syllogism.

R1: All prime ministers have cheesy feet.

R2: Gordon Brown is a prime minister.

C: Gordon Brown has cheesy feet.

If we rewrote this argument, such that we labelled R2 as C (and C as R2) it would still be an argument. But it would no longer be a valid argument because prime ministers are not the only people with cheesy feet. Candidates can have fun playing with this form of argument at any point in the course.

g) Two statements expressing opinion/redefining the past. It is possible that the second sentence might give us some reason to accept the first. This is a very borderline case.

h) This example lies on the boundary between explanation and argument. It is open to interpretation whether it is explaining why we have to treat different kinds of claim in different ways or whether it is an argument persuading us that we should treat different kinds of claim in different ways. My own view is that it is an explanation and not subject to persuasive argument. At this stage, you will find it useful to discuss this boundary with the more able students, but this kind of distinction goes beyond the requirements of Unit 1.

i) Argument. Students may enjoy exploring Descartes' ideas.

R: I think,

C: therefore I am.

1.5 Extension

1. Cyclists should not be allowed on the road.

2. They are dangerous/they are rude/they seem to believe that they are superior to us.

3. No. It's a reason for drivers to be fed up with cyclists but not a reason why cyclists should not be allowed on the road.

4. BikeTastic's response is not an argument. No claim is supported by the other claims. The poor behaviour of motorists (described in the second sentence) does not support the claim that they 'have less right to be on the road than we do'. On a generous reading, the last two sentences can be read as a short argument within the rant. 'R: They are there for cars. C: In any case, bikes don't need to stop at red lights.' But this is unconnected from the other opinions that have been expressed.

5. BikeTastic's blog gives some support to all three of Angry Driver's claims. He is rude ('fat backsides'), seems to feel superior, ('have less right to be on the road than we do') and is probably dangerous ('bikes don't need to stop at red lights').

6. Students can come up with their own ideas here. Teachers should push with questions: 'How does that give me a reason to improve facilities for cyclists?' 'Why do you think that?' to encourage students to push their own ideas further.

1.1 Foundation

1. **Which of the following are arguments?**

   a) Mud fights are really good fun. We had lots of mud fights in the park last summer. It rained a lot last summer.

   b) GCSE grades keep getting better. Teachers are using more interesting teaching methods. Students are more motivated to succeed.

   c) Young girls often do not eat breakfast. Breakfast is the most important meal of the day. Sausages and beans is a healthier breakfast than sugary cereals.

   d) It is a really good idea to do something creative. Activities like art and music can help you relax. Being creative is a way of expressing your real feelings.

   e) People who knock on the door trying to sell you new windows or take your money for charity are really annoying. People who phone up while you are eating dinner never shut up. You can't even be rude to them.

2. **For each of the following, decide whether to insert *because* or *therefore* into the gap.**

   a) *The Wizard of Oz* is on at our local theatre. I like singing, 'Ding Dong the wicked witch is dead!' at the top of my voice. But _____ the lead role is played by an ageing comic who wasn't even funny in the 1980s, I won't be going to see the production.

   b) We have to meet next week. I can't do Monday or Tuesday. You are in Canada from Thursday. _____ we had better meet on Wednesday.

   c) Children are more likely to eat fruit and veg if they see people they respect enjoying them. _____ it is important to eat plenty of fruit and veg to keep healthy, adults should eat healthily in front of their children.

   d) Meat murders the environment _____ a kilogram of beef is responsible for more pollution than driving for 3 hours while leaving all the lights on at home. _____ becoming a veggie is good for the environment.

1.2 Core

1. Which of the following are arguments?

   a) If you are learning to play the cello, long fingernails prevent you pressing the strings down properly. This means you can't hit the notes. So it sounds horrible.

   b) Technological change should be embraced with open arms. Technology has changed an enormous amount over the last 100 years. Technology such as CCTV can restrict our privacy.

   c) Attendance at Glastonbury increased again this year. There was a range of musical attractions, from Tina Turner to Pink. Campers once again had to endure torrential rain to listen to lead attractions. Kayla North, of Bristol, said the festival was excellent.

   d) It would be good to hear more about the achievements of young people on the news. We hear so much about yobs, but most young people work hard, contribute to society, volunteer for charity, and are kind, giving and loving. They deserve to have their achievements praised.

2. When you identify an argument in Worksheet 1.1, decide what the conclusion is and what reasons are given to support it.

3. Match the conclusions below (1–5) to the reasons (A–P) that best support them. Some conclusions might need two reasons. Some reasons do not need to be used.

Conclusions

1. I should switch to History AS from Sociology.

2. The college really shouldn't have painted the walls orange.

3. I should vote for Dave as social secretary in the SU elections.

4. I should buy an Apple iPhone.

5. I should study Media Technology at uni instead of becoming a plumber.

Reasons

A I am really interested in becoming a sound engineer.

B He is really good looking.

C I flushed my iPod down the loo.

D I miss learning about the way things used to be.

E It makes the teacher look ill.

(continued overleaf)

1.2 Core

(*cont.*)

F He organises fantastic parties.

G The colour gives me a headache.

H My Sociology teacher was horrible to me.

I I don't like Social Theory.

J Lots of us find it really difficult to concentrate in the orange glare.

K I don't want to unblock other people's loos.

L I want to be on TV.

M It's the latest gadget.

N I can't do maths.

O I don't have a phone or an MP3 player at the moment.

P I earned lots of money over the summer.

1.3 Extension

1. **Which of the following are arguments?**

   a) Being extremely clever and mathematically minded is no longer enough to get you a computing job. Companies want graduates who understand management and business systems and can explain things clearly to customers. Some universities are offering 'charm school' to computer science students to improve their social skills.

   b) Traditional computer scientists are losing business for companies. No one can understand what they say. They tend to be expert on cutting edge technology but unsure about older business systems, such as COBOL, which companies actually use.

   c) Microsoft has bewailed the shortage of women working in the computing industry. Pregnancy is a particular problem, as women returning from maternity leave have lost touch with fast-moving technology.

   d) New IT and Computing Science courses ought to include business management and communication skills courses. Businesses want people who are technically competent and can also work in a team. They are especially keen to recruit graduates who can explain complex systems in terms that clients can understand.

   e) Putting more emphasis on social skills will address the imbalance between men and women in the IT industry. Women are often better at communicating and negotiating than men. IT courses have always attracted a proportion of males who fit the standard stereotype of the nerd or geek.

   f) Demand for IT professionals has steadily increased since 2004. The number of students on IT courses has steadily declined since 2000. Twenty per cent of IT students are female. It is no longer acceptable that universities churn out IT graduates with excellent software skills but no social ability.

2. **Identify the conclusion and reasons in the arguments.**

1.4 Extension

1. **Which of the following are arguments?**

   a) Snow is not white. Colour is something that we see, not something that is there in the object. If no one is looking, there is no one to see any whiteness in, for example, snow, so there is no whiteness.

   b) I'm going to get a cup of tea. I need to clear my head and get some more ideas before I carry on thinking about this. My head feels like it is tied in knots.

   c) Snow doesn't exist independently of us. It is only snow because we say it is snow. So snow isn't snow.

   d) Two plus two. Therefore, four.

   e) A circle isn't a circle. It is actually a polygon with so many sides you can't see them.

   f) Gordon Brown has cheesy feet. All prime ministers have cheesy feet. Gordon Brown is a prime minister.

   g) The past does not exist. The past is a fiction designed to account for the discrepancy between my immediate physical sensations and my frame of mind.

   (*Life, the Universe and Everything*, Douglas Adams)

   h) Claims have different natures. 'Peas are green' is importantly different from 'Peas are nasty'. Both are different from 'God is good'. So we have to treat different kinds of claims in different ways.

   i) I think, therefore I am.

2. **When you identify an argument, decide what the conclusion is and what reasons are given to support it.**

3. **Choose two conclusions from the above, and give two extra reasons to support them. Consider carefully what makes something a reason that would support a conclusion.**

1.5 Extension

Read the blog and answer the questions that follow.

> `Angry Driver:` Cyclists should not be allowed on the road. First of all, they are dangerous. For example, they jump red lights, ride the wrong way down the carriageway, and fail to use lights at night. Second, they are rude. Last night a cyclist used my car to push off against and then swore at me when I objected. Third, they seem to believe that they are superior to us motorists.

> `BikeTastic:` Angry Driver demonstrates exactly what is wrong with Britain's roads. Motorists, who drive gas-guzzling heaps of world-killing metal, can't be bothered to move their fat backsides and routinely compete to bruise most cyclists, have less right to be on the road than we do. It is unjust that they complain about our behaviour when they are so clearly the dangerous road hogs round here. In any case, bikes don't need to stop at red lights. They are there for cars.

1. Identify the conclusion of Angry Driver's argument.

2. Identify two reasons Angry Driver gives to support his argument.

3. Does Angry Driver's third reason really support his conclusion?

4. Is BikeTastic's blog contribution an argument?

5. Do any of the claims in BikeTastic's blog give support to Angry Driver's claims?

6. Think of examples to illustrate your reasons.

2 Counter-assertions, counter-arguments, hypothetical reasoning and assumptions

CHAPTER OVERVIEW

In this chapter students will learn to identify the following argument components: counter-assertions, counter-arguments and hypothetical reasoning. They will consider the nature of different claims. They will begin to work on argument notation. Students will be introduced to assumptions, which are the unstated parts of an argument.

Components and their nature

This chapter extends the skill of analysis to include additional parts of an argument. These components help to give colour and subtlety to an argument.

Because argument is persuasive, and because we are dealing with everyday reasoning, it is likely that people will come to different conclusions about matters of interest or importance. This means that considering – and rejecting – how people will support a different, or opposing, conclusion is an important part of supporting your own conclusion.

A counter-assertion is the inclusion of a part of the opposing argument, without citing the supporting grounds or logical consequences. A counter-argument includes at least one reason and a conclusion that differ from the author's own. In both cases, the inclusion of a counter-position allows the author to seem to have taken opposing views into account. The author might acknowledge part of the counter-position: 'That may be true, but it doesn't mean that …'; alternatively they may show that this position is misguided or wrong. At this stage, students only need to recognise counter-argument, but it will be useful later if you encourage them to start thinking about how they might give reasons to show that a counter-assertion or counter-argument is wrong, or doesn't undermine their own conclusions. (Just dismissing a counter-argument, having mentioned it, suggests that you can't respond to it.)

Counter-arguments, like arguments, consist of reasons and conclusions, or 'claims'. There are different sorts of claim such as opinion, fact or principle. One particular form of claim considered in this chapter is a hypothetical claim, which takes the form 'if this, then that' to make a prediction.

Assumptions

Assumptions are slightly different from any other argument component that candidates are asked to identify, because they exist only as logical gaps in the reasoning. But it is their very absence from the written part of the argument that makes identifying them so important and difficult. It is often precisely the hidden part of someone's attempts to persuade us that we most need to know about.

Argument notation

Student Book Chapter 2 pages 16–37
Specification 3.1.1 bullet 7

Argument notation is a useful tool for students to become familiar with. Rather than giving students additional exercises to practise notation, you might find it most useful to expect them to get into the habit of using it. Answers to activities will normally use this notation.

Learning objectives

- Use common notation for the component parts of an argument.
- Understand and use counter-assertions and counter-arguments.
- Understand the nature of different claims.
- Recognise simple hypothetical reasoning.
- Understand the meaning of the term 'assumptions'.
- Identify assumptions in arguments.
- Phrase assumptions with precision.

Common problems

When asked to identify hypothetical reasoning, students tend to go blank, or pick any sentence with an 'if' in it.

When asked to identify assumptions, many students find it difficult to let go of their prior understanding of 'assumption' as something that is stated but unfounded and might not be true.

Students who do attempt to identify missing steps in the reasoning often miss the mark by making their assumption too strong or too weak.

Strategies

Again, repetition is the key to students understanding the meaning of the terms 'assumption' and 'hypothetical reasoning'. To reinforce this understanding, especially for less able students, ask students to define a key term at the beginning of every lesson. Play key terms bingo. Use the key terms grid (Worksheet 4.2). Show students the definitions, then ask them to fill in the words in groups and award points.

Suggested activities

Try the following technique with the key terms introduced in this chapter and to revise those from Chapter 1. It can be effective as a filler or 5-minute fun revision slot (with points or other suitable bribery available) later in the course too.

Games for memory

Cover words or definitions on an OHP with a cardboard cut-out of an animal – perhaps a fierce bear (these can be traced from children's books). Ask students which critical thinking key term(s) the bear has (or has not) eaten today. As more terms are learned, you might show students up to ten terms for a few seconds, then allow the bear to 'eat' them. Give students a minute to write down as many of the ten as they can remember. This trains their memories too, which is useful. To extend this activity, ask students to give you the definitions of the words rather than the words themselves. Of course, this can be done as a 'straight' activity without the bear, especially if your students are on their dignity in a new college. But the bear can allow even very bright students to play and engage the creative parts of their brains, and to laugh (often an aid to learning).

Class activities

The assumptions we look at in Critical Thinking are, specifically, gaps in the logic of the argument. They are often unstated reasons. Remind students to ask: 'What else do I have to agree with if I am going to accept the conclusion?' Use the worksheet activities one by one as class activities until students become confident.

Guidance to worksheet activities

Although this unit is not, strictly speaking, about identifying conclusions, all the exercises ask students to identify the conclusion. This is such an important skill that there cannot be too much practice. Also, if students are looking for a counter-assertion, they need to know 'counter to what'. If they are looking for an assumption – a missing reason that has to be accepted if the conclusion is to be accepted – it helps if they know what the conclusion is.

2.1 Foundation

1.
 i) a) C: I think I would like to study in Manchester.
    b) CA: I have been advised to apply to L.S.E.
 ii) a) C: It did make sense to just buy a cheap desk.
     b) CA: I thought we should buy some funky bedroom furniture.
 iii) a) C: I should look for an apprenticeship.
      b) CA: (My friends tell me) I would be better off going to uni.

2.
 i) a) C: I had better stay at home.
    b) HR: If I do go out, I will spend lots of money.
 ii) a) C: I'd better buy some King of the Jungle aftershave.
     b) HR: If I get it wrong, she will think I'm a hopeless geek.
 iii) a) C: I'll try to talk to him about it.
      b) HR: If I tell him so, I might hurt his feelings.

2.2 Core

1.
   i) a) C: I'd better get the bus.
      b) CAss: I don't really want to spend £2.30 on the bus fare.
   ii) a) C: We should just be sensible about being in the sun.
       b) and c) CArg: R – Strong sun can give you skin cancer; C – You should never sunbathe or go out in afternoon sun.

2.
   i) a) C: It is a stupid idea to actually do this (take CDs from the shop without paying for them).
      b) CAss: Although it is very tempting to take CDs from the shop without paying for them
      c) N/A.
      d) If you take CDs from the shop without paying for them you could get a criminal record.
   ii) a) It was the right decision (to buy a clarinet).
       b) Although I really wanted to learn to play the oboe.
       c) N/A.
       d) If I had bought an oboe I might have given up quite quickly.

2.3 Extension

1. C: Astrology should be accorded its place as a science.

2. CAss: There are those who accuse astrologers of fraudulence and mystification.

3. HR: If you have your horoscope drawn properly using your precise place and time of birth, you will find that there are much closer links.

4. No, it does not support the conclusion well. It assumes its conclusion to be true in order for the reasoning to make sense (see Unit 2 Chapter 11), redefines 'evidence', misunderstands scientific evidence, ignores coincidence … .

4. goes beyond the demands of Unit 1. In the exam students will only be asked whether the reasons and evidence support the conclusion. But the exam is only the test – the teaching can place different and interesting demands on students as well.

2.4 Foundation

1.
   i) a) C: I should buy them for myself.
      b) A: I can afford them.
   ii) a) C: Laura killed Dave.
       b) A: Dave was knifed. A: Laura used the knife. A: Laura did not come in and pick up the knife after Dave was killed.
   iii) a) C: Women will find you attractive.
        b) A: You are not repulsive in every other way. A: A statement that is generally true is true of a specific individual.
   iv) a) C: I'll see you then.
       b) A: Your train will run on time.

2.
a) Because. b) Although, because. c) Although, therefore. d) Some may argue that, therefore. e) Although, therefore.

2.5 Core

i) a) C: Carlo Adducci should encourage young singers.
   b) A: He is at the top of his profession.

ii) a) C: We should encourage projects like this in deprived areas of the UK.
    b) A: The project is achieving its (social) aims.

iii) a) C: You should go.
     b) A: You have never heard a boy band play live.

iv) a) C: You should become a veggie.
    b) A: It is morally wrong to eat/kill sweet, furry animals.

v) a) C: So I'll carry on enjoying my rare steak.
   b) A: If something is natural that makes it morally acceptable/something natural cannot be morally wrong. Something being natural is a good enough reason to keep doing it.

vi) a) C: So I should get the clothes.
   b) A: I don't want to stand out/there's something wrong with standing out.

vii) a) C: The government should stop spending our money on this 'art'.
   b) A: The government should only spend 'our' money on things we like/don't moan about.

2.1 Foundation

1. Read the arguments i) to iii) below and:

   a) identify the main conclusion

   b) identify the counter-assertion.

   i) Although I have been advised to apply to L.S.E., I think I would like to study in Manchester. The university has a really good department for Management Studies. It also has a good reputation for looking after students. Manchester has a great social scene.

   ii) We went to a furniture showroom yesterday. I thought we should buy some funky bedroom furniture. But we only went for a desk and, anyway, I'm going to uni soon, and Mum and Dad don't have that much money. So it did make sense to just buy a cheap desk.

   iii) I should look for an apprenticeship. I've seen a good one laminating millionaires' boats. My friends tell me I would be better off going to uni, but I like making things, I like boats, I want to earn money and I hate book learning.

2. Read the arguments i) to iii) below and:

   a) identify the main conclusion

   b) identify the hypothetical reasoning.

   i) I want to go out tonight. If I do go out, I will spend lots of money. I am saving for a car. I also have lots of work to do before tomorrow. I had better stay at home.

   ii) I have met a really nice girl, Emily. She has agreed to go for a coffee with me after college. If I get it wrong, she will think I'm a hopeless geek. I want her to think I'm masculine, interesting and attractive. I'd better buy some King of the Jungle aftershave.

   iii) There's a really kind, sensitive and funny boy who gets the same bus as me. Since I agreed to go for coffee with him, he's been acting like a total moron and wearing foul aftershave. I fancied him more the way he was before. If I tell him so, I might hurt his feelings. But I miss the way he was before. So I'll try to talk to him about it.

2.2 Core

1. Read the two arguments below and:

   a) identify the main conclusion

   b) identify any counter-argument or counter-assertion

   c) if there is a counter-argument, analyse it into reason and conclusion.

   i) It's raining really hard. I don't really want to spend £2.30 on the bus fare, but if I get the bus I won't get wet. It's miserable sitting through lessons soaking wet, and I've got Mrs Richards this morning. She's never very sympathetic. I'd better get the bus.

   ii) Some may argue that you should never sunbathe or go out in afternoon sun because strong sun can give you skin cancer. However, some exposure to the sun is necessary. We need the sun to help us make Vitamin D, which prevents bone problems like rickets. Sunshine on the retina also helps us make the feel-good chemical seratonin. And it is burning that increases the risk of cancer. So, we should just be sensible about being in the sun.

2. In the following arguments:

   a) identify the main conclusion

   b) identify any counter-argument or counter-assertion

   c) if there is a counter-argument, analyse it into reason and conclusion.

   d) identify any hypothetical reasoning.

   i) Although it is very tempting to take CDs from the shop without paying for them, it is a stupid idea to actually do this. If you take CDs from the shop without paying for them you could get a criminal record. having a criminal record can affect your job prospects.

   ii) Although I really wanted to learn to play the oboe, I bought a clarinet last week. This was the right decision. A beginner's oboe costs £800 whereas a beginner's clarinet costs £360. It is also easier for a beginner to make a nice sound with a clarinet than an oboe, which can sound like a quacking duck when played inexpertly. I am easily discouraged. If I had bought an oboe I might have given up quite quickly. This would have been a waste of lots of money.

2.3 Extension

Read the passage and answer the questions below.

Astrology should be accorded its place as a science. Science looks at evidence and draws conclusions from it. This is what astrologers do. Over millennia we have looked at the evidence in the stars, and the evidence of how the stars influence our lives on Earth. Then we draw conclusions which we use to make predictions. There are those who accuse astrologers of fraudulence and mystification, but this is totally unjust. People should always be prepared to find out about things before dismissing them. Just consider how often you have read in horoscopes that the dominance of Mercury in your astral house will lead to difficulties with money, only to find that you are indeed having problems with money. If you have your horoscope drawn properly using your precise place and time of birth, you will find that there are much closer links. For example, mine was done by a complete stranger when I was 14. It gave strong indications that there was a close relationship with a dominant male, and indeed, I have always enjoyed a strong, loving relationship with my father.

1. Identify the main conclusion of the passage.

2. Identify the counter-assertion.

3. Identify the hypothetical reasoning.

4. Do you think this reasoning gives strong support to the conclusion? Why?

2.4 Foundation

1. Read the arguments i) to iv) below and:

   a) identify the main conclusion

   b) identify any unstated assumptions.

   i) I really like those dangly earrings. I should buy them for myself.

   ii) Laura was found standing next to Dave's body with a knife in her hand. Laura killed Dave.

   iii) Women find men with deep voices attractive. You have a deep voice, so women will find you attractive.

   iv) Your train is due to arrive at 6.30. I'll see you then.

2. In the following arguments, choose the appropriate argument indicator from the list below. Insert it in the gap.

   because   although   some may argue that   therefore

   a) _____ we are running late, we should hurry up.

   b) _____ it is getting dark, we should go for a walk _____ it will do us good.

   c) There is a frail looking man in the seat I have reserved on this busy train. _____ my feet ache and I have bags of shopping, it would feel wrong to make him stand up instead. _____ I will stand.

   d) There is going to be another concert this summer trying to combat global warming. _____ this is just a marketing ploy to sell more tickets to a concert full of rock and pop has-beens. However, global warming is a really important issue. If celebrities can make young people think about the way they live and use fewer resources, the concert will have achieved its purpose. _____ we should support it.

   e) _____ it may be for a good cause, everyone will drive or fly to that concert and use up huge amounts of fossil fuel. _____ it will defeat its purpose.

2.5 Core

1. Read the arguments i) to vii) below and:

   a) identify the main conclusion

   b) identify the assumptions.

   i) Carlo Adducci should encourage young singers. People at the top of their profession should do some good for those just starting out.

   ii) In Venezuela there is a project to get deprived kids playing musical instruments. It is intended to improve their self-confidence, prevent them from becoming involved in drugs and crime, and give them better life chances. In 2007 they came to the UK and really impressed an audience at the Royal Albert Hall as part of the summer Proms season. We should encourage projects like this in deprived areas of the UK.

   iii) Everybody should hear a boy band playing live at least once in their lives. McFly are playing at Wembley next year. You should go.

   iv) You don't like doing things that are morally wrong. Meat is made of dead animals. Animals are sweet and furry when they're alive and they have beautiful eyes. You should become a veggie.

   v) Men are hunters. They always have been. It's natural. So I'll carry on enjoying my rare steak.

   vi) All my friends are starting to listen to emo music and wear emo clothes. I'm not really sure it's my scene. I'll stand out if I don't join in. So I should get the clothes.

   vii) The government and local councils spend a lot of money on sculpture and other art to go in public places. There's Millennium Square in Bristol. The huge table and chair on Hampstead Heath. The squiggly wire arrangement covered in pigeon poo in your local town. No one really notices these, except to moan about them. The government should stop spending our money on this 'art'.

3 Identifying evidence and examples

CHAPTER OVERVIEW

In this chapter, students will learn how to identify evidence in an argument, and identify different forms of evidence including research data, statistics, etc. They will learn to understand how evidence is used in reasoning and begin to evaluate the reliability of evidence by considering sample size, data collection methods, etc.

Evidence and examples

Student Book Chapter 3 pages 38–51
Specification pp9–10 Section 3.1.1 bullets 3, 7 and 8

The first tasks covered in this chapter are identifying evidence and examples and recognising different kinds of evidence. These tasks come under AO 1 'Analyse argument'. Students should find these tasks relatively easy. Questioning the reliability of evidence in appropriate ways comes under AO 2 'Evaluate argument'. This is more challenging for some students. It is important that students evaluate the nature of the evidence and the way it was gathered in order to decide whether it is reliable. Simple disagreement with the evidence, of the form 'That's not true', is not what critical thinkers are looking for.

In Unit 1, we are concerned with how evidence is gathered, and whether it is reliable. In Chapters 5 and 6 we will move on to consider whether it is plausible and credible. In Unit 2 we will consider how the evidence is used in an argument.

Learning objectives

- Understand what is meant by evidence.
- Understand how evidence is used in reasoning.
- Identify different forms of evidence.
- Understand how numerical data and statistics are used and misused, as evidence.
- Identify where further clarification of evidence is needed.

Common problems

Students are inclined to take evidence as solid proof and not question it.

Students are inclined to disagree with the evidence rather than evaluate its reliability.

Strategies

Keep questioning evidence. Keep highlighting that if the evidence is unreliable, it cannot 'prove' anything.

Remind students that we are not disagreeing with facts.

Suggested activities

Group work

Ask students to find evidence from other subjects and the media. Put them in groups to question it using the questions suggested in the Student Book, Chapter 3 (page 51) and below.

- Is this evidence meaningful?
- Who funded the survey or research?
- What was the size of any sample?
- Was the sample representative?
- How was any survey conducted?
- When was the survey carried out?
- Are examples typical and relevant?

Elicit further questions that can be asked; give points to interesting questions.

3 Identifying evidence and examples

Ask students to make pairs cards with the names of different kinds of evidence, definitions and examples of evidence (which may come from their own research).

Whole class work

Present students with evidence on topical issues; this may be a graph or table from a magazine, a percentage or the results of a survey. Ask them how reliable this information is. Remind them to use the questions overleaf to help them make this judgement.

Guidance to worksheet activities

3.1 Foundation

1.

a) This is research data (using numerical data), reported in a national newspaper.

b) Numerical data containing estimates, prediction and average.

c) Average. Account of events.

2.

a) Ev: The number of cohabiting couples has grown by around 60%. Percentage (taken from survey, but this may not be clear from activity). Questions: From when to when? What are the raw figures? Are cohabiting couples a significant percentage of the total?

b) Ev: There are now 2.6 million lone-parent families. Numerical. Questions: Where does the information come from? How has lone-parent family been defined?

c) Ev: According to the last census, nearly 10% of people who are single after the age of 75 are in a nursing home compared with 1% of those who are married. Percentages taken from a census, which is a survey of everyone (in theory). Questions: How does the census understand 'single'? Does it include widowed or divorced, or does it mean never married? These questions can be clarified. Is it reasonable to assume that what is true of relationships of people who are old today will be the case for those who are young today? There is no definite answer to this question, but if you're 90 now, it would have been thought to be wrong to cohabit when you were young, so a committed relationship had to be marriage. Therefore, single people are probably those who did not have relationships rather than those who cohabited. If you're 30 today, cohabitation is normal, so there are people in committed relationships who are not married.

d) Ev: 'In my dream I'm standing at my mother's sink,' says Liliana, 36. 'I am back in Brazil and have spilt milk all over her kitchen. I am embarrassed and she is trying to clean up after me.' Anecdotal evidence.

Ev: 'Dreams are invariably personal and idiosyncratic,' says Dr Roderick Orner of the British Psychological Society. Expert opinion.

Questions: Is the anecdotal evidence relevant? Can it be generalised? (No.) What is the expert evidence based on? Does the expert have good grounds for believing this?

3.2 Core

1.

a) Fear, insecurity, frustration, love, dependence and powerlessness (examples of emotions).

b) Including 'Yeah whatever'; 'I'm no good at anything'; fixed stereotypes of themselves; total confusion leading to inconsistency such as ranting about consumerism and demanding the latest mobile in the same breath. (All of these are examples of stages of identity struggle. The last part is an example of inconsistency – an example within an example.

c) A parent's decision not to allow the teenager to go out is perceived as lack of trust (examples of fraught moments).

2.

a) 400 is not an enormous sample, but it should be big enough to include a variety of types. As they were all students they may not be representative of the population. The research is designed to dispel the commonly held belief that women talk more than men. It may be characteristic of male students that they are more talkative than the average male (or the women may have been quieter than the average non-student female). We do not know for how many days the students wore the microphones, or whether they were conscious of having the microphones and thus altered their behaviour. The average figure may cover up huge variations, so more information is required. Therefore, we cannot be sure that the information is wholly reliable – but it seems to provide a good guide.

b) The only thing we know about this survey is that it was conducted by a company with 'Internet' in the title, which may indicate that they want to find that the Internet plays an important role (vested interest, see Chapter 5 in the Student Book). It is therefore hard to make judgements about its reliability.

c) None of the evidence in this passage seems reliable. It is plausible that singles want help finding a partner, and that they might be influenced by the South Asian and Arab model of marriage mediation, but the information we have is generalisation with no source. The anecdotal evidence is vague and cannot be relied on, although it does seem to match experience. What it does not tell us, is whether arranged marriages could last longer than love marriages, given our high expectations.

d) The Office for National Statistics ought to be really reliable. But we don't actually know how it collects its data. Is this an estimate based on a survey or sample? Or is it a count of how many men declare themselves to be home fathers?

3.3 Core

1. It is not an argument. It is an account.

2. 'The fire brigade led us out to where the streets had been cordoned off and we waited there for about 3 hours. They said there was a chemical smell and I remember saying to someone that maybe the smell was the chillies.'

   'I was making a nam prik pao, a spicy dip with extra hot chillies that are deliberately burnt. But it doesn't smell like chemicals. I'm a bit confused.'

3. '800 false alarms.'

4. This is probably an unusual example of a false alarm. Most are likely to have been triggered by threats rather than burning food.

5. Discuss this with your class. There is no single right answer.

3 Identifying evidence and examples　　　　　　　　　　　　　　　　OCR AS Critical Thinking

3.1 Foundation

1. **What kinds of evidence are used in the following passages?**

   a) A study by the Tobacco Central Collaborating Centre in Warwick, funded by Cancer Research UK, has found that staff in 40 pubs, bars and restaurants have four times less cotinine (a metabolic byproduct of nicotine) in their blood.

   b) Changing a 60W traditional lightbulb to an 11W low-energy lightbulb will save the average householder £8.58 per lightbulb per year, 30Kg of CO_2 and save two trees.

   c) Police were called to a comprehensive school where pupils had walked out of class and set fire to their school blazers in a protest against new rules requiring them to wear uniforms. The decision to reintroduce the black blazers was made by the school council and was popular with parents despite them costing an average of £34.

   (*The Times*, 3 October 2007)

2. **Read the texts and answer the questions below.**

   a) It is difficult to generalise about cohabiting couples, who may include people who are about to marry, those who oppose marriage and those who are just testing the strength of their relationship, which has become more acceptable in the last 30 years in the UK. The number of cohabiting couples has grown by around 60%, according to a survey.

   b) There are increasing numbers of lone-parent families. There are now 2.6 million lone-parent families.

   c) Cohabitation is growing in younger age groups. According to the last census, nearly 10% of people who are single after the age of 75 are in a nursing home compared with 1% of those who are married. As the younger age group gets older there could be a larger problem of care provision if the relationships don't develop into marriage-like commitments.

   d) Today there are nearly as many interpretations of dreams as there are dreams. 'In my dream I'm standing at my mother's sink,' says Liliana, 36. 'I am back in Brazil and have spilt milk all over her kitchen. I am embarrassed and she is trying to clean up after me.' Freud saw dreams as the path to our subconscious, consisting of symbols and suppressed desires. Jung thought dreams were the expression of certain universal symbols. 'Dreams are invariably personal and idiosyncratic,' says Dr Roderick Orner of the British Psychological Society.

   (*Psychologies*, November 2007, p. 80)

3. Identify the evidence used in each passage.

4. What kind of evidence is it?

5. What questions might you ask about this evidence?

3.2 Core

1. **Identify the examples in the following passages.**

   a) Teenagers can be difficult to live with as they surge between different raging emotions such as fear, insecurity, frustration, love, dependence and powerlessness.

   b) Teenagers' apparently irrational moodiness is blamed on hormones, but the real cause may be their own uncertainty about who they are. Most teenagers go through several stages of identity struggle, including 'Yeah whatever'; 'I'm no good at anything'; fixed stereotypes of themselves; total confusion leading to inconsistency such as ranting about consumerism and demanding the latest mobile in the same breath. Eventually each individual finds a way of being that works for them.

   c) Almost all parent–teenager relationships have fraught moments – when, for example, a parent's decision not to allow the teenager to go out is perceived as lack of trust. But quarrels between parents and teenagers do not mean it is a bad relationship. It can just be a positive move towards a more adult relationship, in which both parent and teenager recognise the other as a mature human being.

2. **Look at the evidence. Is it reliable (sample size, methods of collecting, etc.)?**

   a) Common belief holds that women talk more than men. Matthias R. Mehl at the University of Arizona tested how many words men and women speak each day. He used 400 students wearing electronic recorders. He reports in *Science* that both the male and female volunteers spoke an average of 16,000 words a day.

   (*Psychologies*, November 2007, pp. 90–93)

   b) A 2005 survey by the Pew Internet and American Life Project showed that 15% of US adults (30 million people) knew someone who'd had a serious relationship with, or married, a person they had met online, and 31% knew someone who had used an online dating service. Today, online introductions are the new norm.

   c) More and more singles want help finding a partner, whether that comes from friends, family, websites and now, even professional services. These singles are influenced by their South Asian and Arab friends, whose parents and relatives mediate marriages for them. Statistics are hard to come by, but anecdotal evidence seems to suggest that these arranged marriages will often outlast 'love matches'. Proponents of these unions refer to the high divorce rates in the West as proof that love alone does not guarantee a stable and happy marriage.

   (*Psychologies*, November 2007, p. 101)

   d) The number of home fathers is increasing. In 2007 there were 200,000 of them according to the Office for National Statistics.

3.3 Core

Read the text and answer the questions that follow.

Shoppers dive for cover as chef's eye-watering chilli sauce causes a terror alert

For 3 hours a mysterious cloud of acrid smoke hovered over some of London's busiest streets. As shoppers ran coughing and spluttering for cover, police sealed off three roads and evacuated homes and businesses in the heart of Soho, fearing a chemical attack or a dangerous toxic leak.

Firefighters wearing specialist breathing equipment entered the deserted streets to seek out the source. Soon after 7pm they emerged from the smoke carrying a huge cooking pot containing about 9lb of smouldering dried chillies.

Supranee Yodmuang, the waitress on duty, said: 'The fire brigade led us out to where the streets had been cordoned off and we waited there for about 3 hours. They said there was a chemical smell and I remember saying to someone that maybe the smell was the chillies.'

Chalemchai Tangjariyapoon, the chef, said: 'I was making a nam prik pao, a spicy dip with extra hot chillies that are deliberately burnt. But it doesn't smell like chemicals. I'm a bit confused.'

Sue Wasboonma, the owner, said: 'I think the smoke didn't go up into the sky because of the rain and the heavy air. We are very proud of this dish. The customers love it.'

There have been something like 800 false alarms triggered by fears of chemical terrorist attacks in the last year.

(*The Times*, Wednesday, 3 October 2007 – except last sentence)

1. Is this passage an argument?

2. Identify two pieces of eyewitness evidence in the passage.

3. Identify a piece of numerical evidence.

4. Do you think this incident was a typical example of a false alarm?

5. Do you think the police were right to evacuate this busy area? Why?

4 Analysing and evaluating reasoning

CHAPTER OVERVIEW

In this chapter, students will analyse longer passages using the skills of identifying argument components that they have developed in Chapters 1–3. They will also begin to evaluate reasoning in longer passages, by explaining whether reasons support the conclusion.

Analysing longer arguments

Students identify familiar argument components in longer passages. This is a good opportunity to revisit concepts and ensure that students have a firm grip on them. You can also work towards exam-style answers.

Evaluating long arguments

Student Book Chapter 4 pages 52–63
Specification p10 Section 3.1.1 bullets 7, 10, 11 and 12

This is where evaluation of the logical link between reasons and conclusions appears for the first time in the Student Book. However, it is very basic evaluation, barely extended from the analytical skills students used in Chapter 1. In order to identify an argument for example, students were effectively evaluating whether given claims provided support for a conclusion.

Learning objectives

- Analyse the structure of longer arguments.
- Understand the link between reasons and conclusions.
- Evaluate how well reasons support conclusions.

Common problems

Students forget to quote argument components when they are identifying them.

Students can struggle to distinguish between evidence and reasons. Many write down evidence when asked to identify reasons.

Students forget that assumptions are unstated; this is the one argument component that they cannot copy from the text in front of them.

Students are inclined to disagree with reasons rather than evaluating the logical link between them and reasons.

Students tend to over-estimate reasons and think that a weak reason can support a strong conclusion.

Students tend to be imprecise and not notice details – words such as *all*, *every*, *never*, *always* – which make a significant difference to the strength and meaning of a claim.

Strategies

Practice and repetition really can help them to make the new concepts of Critical Thinking their own.

Use the key terms grid (Worksheet 4.2 and CD-ROM) to revise and play games. Ask able students to devise games for themselves and others to play.

Remind students that thinking is a skill that can be improved with practice.

Start to encourage students to work with longer passages and to discuss more complex topics. If a student produces a nice, short argument, put the discussion on hold and write the argument down. Ask the whole class to analyse it. Ask whether the reasons support the conclusion. Ask if any assumptions are necessary. Weak students often produce arguments that require assumptions. Using their argument as an example for analysis can be rewarding. By also asking what else they have to agree with, the whole class has practice identifying assumptions, and the weak

4 Analysing and evaluating reasoning

students can be encouraged in a non-threatening way to clarify their ideas.

Model good answers to students orally and in writing. Reward students who produce good answers with points. If you are doing oral work and a student gives a thorough answer or makes a good evaluative point during discussion, write it up and ask students to copy it down. It can sometimes be beneficial to allow students to develop their ideas freely and to re-focus them periodically on the specific analytic and evaluative skills that are tested in the exam. An unremitting diet of exam-style questions can be a bit unrewarding.

Suggested activities

Whole class work

Present the class with a short argument from a newspaper, magazine or website. Identify the conclusion (you might ask the class to do this, or point it out to them). Discuss the issue, and allow students to explore and express their own opinions. Refocus on the text. Ask someone to define 'reason' and correct if necessary. If key terms are on the wall, point them in the right direction. It's not cheating; it's good use of resources. Ask another student to define 'evidence' and correct if necessary. Ask a third how to tell the difference. (Reasons tend to be more general than evidence, which is by definition specific – and if it's got numbers in it, it's normally evidence.)

Ask students to work in pairs to identify the reasons the author uses to support the conclusions. Remind them to find the reasons in the text and quote them.

Ask students what else they might need to accept in order to agree with the conclusion – that is, what is assumed. Remind them of the Critical Thinking definition of 'assumption' if necessary (page 25 of the Student Book and again on Worksheet 4.2).

Present students with some mismatched reasons and conclusions – for example: R: Speed cameras cannot ensure road safety. C: We should no longer use speed cameras. (Just because speed cameras are not enough to ensure road safety doesn't mean they shouldn't be used at all. A better conclusion might be that we should use other measures to ensure road safety as well as speed cameras.)

Return to the article. Ask students whether the reasons give strong support to the conclusion.

Guidance to worksheet activities

4.1 Core

1. C: There are some things that it is unwise to put in your microwave at home.

2. R: Putting the wrong things in your microwave can be messy. R: There are some things that can cause injury to you if you put them in your microwave (NB hypothetical reasoning). R: They may also damage the microwave. (Paragraph 1 explains how a microwave works but does not give reasons why it is unwise to put some things in the microwave.)

3. This is factual evidence from experiments.

4.3 Core

1. We should all get involved (in swishing).

2. The delights of a hard-won payday blowout are too sweet to give up.

3. 75% of waste textiles end up burned or in landfill.

4. Swishing can be much more fun than normal shopping.

5. We have to assume that swishing being more fun is a reason for us all to get involved.

6. If you swish you can live a sustainable lifestyle.

7. This claim is exaggerated and therefore not reasonable. It would be more reasonable to suggest that swishing could contribute to a more sustainable lifestyle – but if you are buying so many clothes that you have some left over to swap before they are unwearable, you are probably using unsustainable amounts of resources.

8. Examples include:

    Ex: Feather Duster has a loyal following.

    Ex: 2007 saw the first mainstream event, a celebrity-backed swap shop sponsored by Visa.

Ex: Virginia Rowe, 31, editor of hip fashion website stylewillsaveus.com.

Ex: The same woman (let's call her, um, me).

Ex: Judy Berger, founder of the clothes swap and resale website, whatsmineisyours.com.

9. This is poorly supported. Although swapping clothes may be less expensive than buying them, it is not clear that you will get value for money. More evidence would be needed. Furthermore, if people like Judy Berger are running swap sites as a full time business, they must be making money out of it. And £2.50 to swap one item for another? You've got the same number of clothes, no guarantee that the new item is of equal value with the old, and you're £2.50 worse off. Remember – it may be true that swishing will satisfy your desire for value for money, but it is poorly supported by this paragraph.

10. The reasons provide grounds for people to get involved but are not strong enough to support the conclusion that we should all get involved.

11. Students might come up with a variety of reasons. Suggestion: it is nicer to own something new; swishing just feeds the unsustainable clothes buying frenzy while making people feel unreasonably virtuous; it would be better to buy a few high quality, ethically sourced items and use them for a sensible length of time.

General discussion

Questions 12–17 invite reflection on the topic rather than the analytical skills that make up most of the Unit 1 Section A exam. Although such reflection will not be tested in the Unit 1 exam, it forms an important part of the process of learning to think critically. It should also help students to maintain an interest and develop their own thoughts at their own level. They can begin to structure their own arguments in preparation for Unit 2.

12. No. It depends on our high-street habit. And the reason given why our high-street habit is not going away, is that the payday blowout is too sweet to give up. Swishing does not represent a payday blowout, but an end of month frugal substitute.

13. No. The clothes have probably still been sourced unethically, paid for inappropriately and will probably still end up on a landfill.

14–17. Discuss.

4 Analysing and evaluating reasoning

OCR AS Critical Thinking

4.1 Core

Read the passage and answer the questions that follow.

There are some things that it is unwise to put in your microwave oven at home. A microwave is a powerful heating device. It uses microwaves, which are made up of a vibrating electric and magnetic field to line up molecules in the material being heated. The field alternates rapidly, causing the molecules to vibrate back and forth. They generate friction, and this heats the material. It works best in liquids because their molecules are more mobile.

Putting the wrongs things in your microwave can be messy, as the following experiments show. First, an egg was placed in a plastic holder in the centre of a microwave oven. The microwave was set to full power and switched on. The egg exploded, covering the oven's walls. Water within the egg had been heated to over 100°C, creating steam. The gas built up until the shell cracked spectacularly under pressure. Second, a bar of soap was heated on full power. The soap expanded, creating a polystyrene-like goo. Soap contains water, fats and trapped air which expand when heated, sometimes to five times the size of the original bar of soap.

There are some things that can cause injury to you if you put them in your microwave. They may also damage the microwave. First, a CD was stood against a cardboard box inside the microwave so it was easy to see what happened when it was heated on full power. It melted into an amorphous* mess. It's basically a disc of plastic with a thin metal coating which absorbs microwave energy. This caused the plastic to melt and partially burn off, releasing noxious smoke. Then a roll of steel wool was heated at full power. The wool glowed like bonfire embers. The electrical charge absorbed by the metal concentrated at the wool's jagged edges. These reached high voltages, leading to flashes of electrical energy, causing fires.

BBC worldwide and the publishers and editors of *Focus* magazine can accept no responsibility for personal injuries or damage to property that may result from experimenting with your microwave oven.

*Amorphous: shapeless, blobby.

(*BBC Focus*, October 2007, pp 52–53)

1. Identify the main conclusion of the argument.

2. Identify three reasons given to support the conclusion.

3. What sort of evidence is used in this argument?

4.2 Core

Argument	Attempt to persuade a reader (or listener) to accept something. An argument must have a conclusion and at least one reason.
Reason	A statement that aims to persuade the reader to accept a conclusion.
Conclusion	Statement supported by reasons.
Counter-assertion	Reason, evidence or conclusion that would oppose the author's conclusion. Normally presented in order to dismiss it and strengthen one's own argument.
Counter-argument	Argument including at least one reason and a conclusion that would oppose the author's conclusion. Normally presented in order to dismiss it and strengthen one's own argument.
Assumption	Missing step in the argument (often a reason). Must be accepted if the conclusion is to be accepted.
Hypothetical reasoning	Claim in the form, 'If … then …' that looks at the consequences that might occur. Prediction.

(continued over)

4.2 Core

(cont.)

Evidence	Specific factual information, which might include examples, statistics, numerical data, estimates, personal observations, statements from witnesses and research or survey data.
Example	Specific, real-life instance that illustrates a point being made.
Analyse	Break an argument down into its component parts and label them as reasons, conclusion, etc. AO 1
Evaluate	Consider how well an argument works. Do the reasons support the conclusion? Is the assumption reasonable? Is the evidence reliable? AO 2
Explanation	Tells us how or why something is the case. Does not attempt to persuade the reader to accept a claim.
Reasoning	The process of thinking through an argument; the reasons that support a conclusion.
Develop your own reasoning	Give reasons to support a conclusion. Write an argument. Use your own ideas. AO 3

4.3 Core

Read the passage and answer the questions below.

Our high-street habit is not going away because the delights of a hard-won payday blowout are too sweet to give up. But recent high-street sweatshop scandals, plus awareness of the fact that 75% of waste textiles end up burned or in landfill, have eroded the feel-good factor of cheap fashion. Fortunately, there's a new way to shop: swishing is the new shopping and we should all get involved. **1**

'Swishing' means swapping. All you need is a bunch of like-minded people, each armed with a bag of clothes to trade. Clothes swapping events have long been common in the USA, and are gaining popularity on this side of the Atlantic and in Australia. Grassroots British parties such as Feather Duster has a loyal following, and summer 2007 saw the first mainstream event, a celebrity-backed swap shop sponsored by Visa. **2**

Swishing can be much more fun than normal shopping. 'It's so nice to see clothes you've loved in the past going to a good home,' says Virginia Rowe, 31, editor of hip fashion website stylewillsaveus.com. She most enjoys the intimate little parties with DJs and a bar. **3**

Until recently fashion was an anomaly: the same woman (let's call her, um, me) who diligently took a cloth bag to the store, tried to shop locally and recycle her waste, would buy cheap, dubiously sourced high-street clothes, knowing full well they would have a shorter shelflife than a lettuce. Swishing is 'eco-fabulous' – if you swish you can live a sustainable lifestyle. **4**

Swishing will satisfy your desire for value for money too. 'People are starting to wake up to swapping as a way of expanding their wardrobe without spending money,' says Judy Berger, founder of the clothes swap and resale website, whatsmineisyours.com. Her clothes swap passion has grown into a full time business, with swaps on the site now overtaking sales, at great value for just £2.50 a swap. **5**

(Jess Cartner-Morley in *Marie Claire*, November 2007)

1. Identify the main conclusion of the argument.

2. Identify the reason given by the author to support the claim: 'Our high-street habit is not going away.'

3. Identify the evidence used in paragraph 1.

4. Identify a reason given in paragraph 3 to support the main conclusion.

5. What has to be assumed for paragraph 3 to support the conclusion?

(continued over)

4.3 Core

(*cont.*)

6. Identify the hypothetical reason in paragraph 4.

7. How reasonable is this claim?

8. Identify three examples used in the article.

9. 'Swishing will satisfy your desire for value for money too.' Paragraph 5. How well is this claim supported?

10. How well do the reasons support the main conclusion?

11. Give two reasons of your own to counter the claim that, 'we should all get involved in swishing'.

General Discussion

12. Does the article really show that swishing will satisfy our high-street habit?

13. Does swishing really answer ethical concerns about high-street fashion?

14. Can fashion ever be ethical? Why?

15. Can feminists be fashionable? Why?

16. How relevant is fashion to men? Support your view.

17. Why is it important to live a sustainable lifestyle?

Section 2 Credibility

Chapter 5	**The credibility criteria**	37
	Worksheet 5.1 Foundation	42
	Worksheet 5.2 Core	43
	Worksheet 5.3 Extension	44
Chapter 6	**Assessing credibility of individuals, organisations and documents**	45
	Worksheet 6.1 Core	51
	Worksheet 6.2 Core	53
	Worksheet 6.3 Extension	56
Unit 1	**Guidance to the Activities**	58

5 The credibility criteria

> **CHAPTER OVERVIEW**
>
> In this chapter, students will learn what 'credibility' means, assess the plausibility, extent and reasonableness of claims, understand and apply criteria for judging credibility and explain how credibility criteria strengthen or weaken claims.

Credibility

Credibility as assessed in Unit 1 is an introduction to basic decision making. Critical Thinking skills are used in the context of making a judgement. The key questions are as follows.

- Who should I believe?
- What should I believe?

The first question is used as a tool for answering the second. We are born with very little knowledge and through our lives we are confronted with a great many claims to knowledge. It can be difficult to decide for ourselves which of these we should accept for ourselves. By looking at the plausibility of the claims and the credibility of the people making them, we can give students the ability to sift through these claims making their own judgements.

This chapter encourages students to use the criteria of plausibility, bias, vested interest, neutrality, expertise, ability to perceive, reputation, corroboration and (in)consistency to judge credibility.

Plausibility of claims

In this chapter, students will consider the criterion of whether a claim is plausible. The other credibility criteria look at the source of a claim in order to judge whether we should trust the source. Plausibility is the only criterion that looks only at the claim and its own nature.

However credible the source of the following claim, we would be inclined not to believe it, because it is rather far-fetched: 'Little green men from Mars were dancing round my garden last night waving their antennae at me.'

We do not know for certain that this is impossible but it also not really plausible.

Corroboration and inconsistency

Student Book Chapter 5 pages 64–85
Specification p11 Section 3.1.2 bullets 1 and 2

Corroboration is a criterion that requires students to compare more than one claim and establish points of agreement. If there is independent agreement between claims from different sources, this makes these claims more credible – that is, more likely to be honest representations, and therefore more believable.

If a number of accounts are consistent with one another – that is, if they could all be true at the same time – this would make them more believable.

Inconsistency could take two forms. There could either be explicit conflict or contradiction between claims. Or there could be a more implicit inconsistency, where two or more claims are made that cannot both (or all) be true at the same time.

If a single source makes inconsistent claims, the source can be judged as not very credible. If inconsistent claims are made by different sources, this will affect the credibility of one or both of them. Students will need to consider this alongside other credibility criteria.

Learning objectives
- Understand what is meant by the term 'credibility'.
- Assess the plausibility, extent and reasonableness of claims.
- Understand and apply criteria for judging credibility.
- Explain how credibility criteria strengthen or weaken claims.

Common problems
Students confuse 'true', 'plausible' and 'credible'.

Strategies
Discuss what 'true' means. We take truth to be some form of objective reality: 'This is what actually happened.'

How do we know what this truth, this objective reality, is? If you have a very able group, you could spend some time researching and discussing these concepts.

We try to find out what is true by considering what is plausible (what could reasonably have been the case) and what is credible (what is believable or reliable).

As ever, key terms and definition games played every so often or as 5-minute fillers can help students to hold these concepts apart.

Suggested activities
Whole class
Write the following claim on the board: 'Your exam includes two written papers and some coursework.' Ask whether this is true. Hopefully students will realise that there is no coursework. Set up a conflict between a confident student and yourself. Point out that it cannot be true both that they have coursework and that they have no coursework.

Ask whether either of the claims could be true, or is plausible. Students should establish that either is plausible. It is not far-fetched to suppose that there might be coursework.

Ask students to consider whom they might be more likely to believe when it comes to the content of an exam, the teacher or another member of class. Consider the credibility criteria. Give points to students who make appropriate points. You should establish that, in general, a teacher would be more credible as having greater expertise.

Ask students what evidence they would need to make a judgement. They may quote people who took the course last year (but the assessment might have changed since then) or you yourself (I might have made a mistake), etc. Someone might suggest a specification. Show them page 20 (Section 4.1) of the specification (available on the OCR website), which outlines the assessment for AS Critical Thinking as having two examinations and no coursework.

This evidence settles the dispute. Although you were credible and plausible, your claim was untrue. The student was less credible, but also plausible, and their claim was true. This should help to separate truth, credibility and plausibility. It also shows the role that reliable evidence can play in settling such a dispute.

Media activities
You may wish to show students an excerpt from *The Royle Family* which shows Ricky Tomlinson as the father giving his typical response to unlikely statements. Students may wish to have some fun thinking up implausible explanations or theories for everyday happenings and contrasting them with more plausible ones.

Show students *Twelve Angry Men*. This is an old film starring Henry Fonda which looks at the evidence in a murder case. They systematically demolish the evidence using credibility criteria.

Group work
Ask students to find evidence – from their other subjects, from newspapers and magazines, from adverts and leaflets. Working in groups, they can assess the reliability of the evidence (using the methods listed in Chapter 3 of the Student Book (page 51)), the plausibility and the credibility, using the criteria. It is worth encouraging them to develop the habit of always explaining why they have made their assessment, because this is where the bulk of the marks are given in the exam. A student who says, 'X has a vested interest' will get fewer marks than a candidate who says, 'X has a vested interest to lie about what he was doing if he was the burglar because he might go to prison'.

Display work

Consider making a display. The leaflets and articles should make a colourful starting point. Students could label them, using a large font (and possibly colour coding) for the credibility criteria and a smaller font for more detailed explanations. Again, points can be given to groups for the most visually appealing display and for the most accurate. If you have time, display is useful for a number of reasons: it uses the creative bits of the brain and engages them in the learning process too, which helps some students learn and remember. Display provides constant visual stimulation which is relevant to ongoing work and can reinforce learning. If it changes regularly, students are more likely to look at it.

Creative group work/peer assessment

Another useful activity is asking students to produce an invented credibility scenario. They should produce the following in groups.
– A situation in which it is unclear what happened.
– Evidence from a number of people or sources, maximum 350 words (editing and drafting skills). There must be evidence that conflicts/is inconsistent and evidence that corroborates. It must be possible to assess the evidence and the sources in terms of plausibility, reputation, ability to see, etc.
– Questions about the plausibility and reasonableness of the claims and the credibility of the people.

Students should also provide a mark scheme. They should consider what possible assessments there are and the marks available. For example, a simple statement, 'Sam's reputation is not very good' might be worth one mark, whereas, 'Sam's claim that she didn't steal the cigarettes is weakened by her reputation as a thief and a smoker' might be worth three or four marks.

Students should hand in their scenarios, typed up on one side of A4 with the mark scheme separate. You can photocopy these and ask students to answer the questions. The group that wrote a question can lead the class through the answers. Give points to groups that produce particularly imaginative or amusing scenarios as well as to those that produce high quality material. Students who are confident and in control leading the class through the answers might also earn points for their group. As an extra challenge, students can evaluate their own questions in the light of the experience of answering them and suggest improvements.

This exercise is a useful point on the way to the exam. It encourages students to think about evidence, what might conflict and what might be plausible. It makes them consider what would be a good answer, and gives them lots of enjoyable practice assessing credibility.

Guidance to worksheet activities

These activities are intended to help students develop the skills they will need in the exam using a variety of different stimuli, not to be exact models of the exam format.

5.1 Foundation

1.

a) It is plausible that Miriam offers such a healing service. It is rather less plausible that it works, because 'Vibrations of Unconditional Love' sounds like a far-fetched attempt to heal.

b) This is probably quite plausible. As a nation we do seem to have a bad shopping habit. There are 55–60 million of us, so it is quite plausible that we might each buy a few things we regret.

c) It is plausible that we might spend a lot less on shopping online than in a shop, because special offers and the sights of the products lined up will not tempt us online. It is also easier to put a virtual cake back on the shelf than a real one.

d) The claim that a particular eye cream will give you younger-looking skin is not particularly plausible, because it is difficult to demonstrate such a claim with evidence.

e) This claim seems quite extreme. But it is not implausible.

2.

a) The factual claims in the advert are plausible. There is no reason to think that they are unreasonable. However, the descriptive claims are less plausible. 'Satisfying' crunch? 'Exlosion' of taste? They are not, of course, intended to be factually plausible, but emotively persuasive. So we need to judge them not as factual claims, but as attempts to manipulate our feelings.

b) The credibility of the claims is weakened by *Vege-Crackles*' vested interest in persuading us to spend money on their new crisps. They may exaggerate or even mislead to do so.

Vege-Crackles have a vested interest to comply with advertising regulations which forbid lies in adverts. So this would make them more likely to be truthful about the factual claims, which strengthens the credibility of these claims.

c) The evidence seems consistent. This makes the claims seem more credible.

d) The factual claims about the amount of fat and the rice content are credible because *Vege-Crackles* have a vested interest to stay on the right side of advertising law.

3.
a) The speaker has a vested interest to lie to avoid a fine or possibly losing their licence, which weakens the credibility of their claims (but does not make them necessarily false).

b) Open this for discussion. We need more information about the speaker, and for preference some additional evidence which would corroborate, or at least be consistent with, their story.

If this person has a history of speeding offences, and five people phoned home but failed to reach them, we would think the person was lying. If they have no history, and perhaps spent time talking to their boss on the landline, or if someone credible saw them watching TV with the curtains open at the relevant time, we would think they were innocent.

5.2 Core

Answers may include the following:

1 a)
- The evidence that 'more than a quarter of Britons identified with the Royle family' seems plausible; it certainly could be the case. This therefore strengthens the credibility of this evidence.
- The evidence comes from an unspecified source, which weakens its credibility slightly, as we do not know how reliable this source is – it may lack expertise, have a poor reputation, or have a vested interest to promote the Royle family. But we do not *know* that it is *not* a reputable, neutral survey.
- The reputation of the *Independent* for quoting reputable sources strengthens the credibility of the document, and therefore also of the evidence quoted in the document.
- So, overall, this claim is quite credible.

b)
- As an accountancy firm, KPMG has the relevant expertise to make this claim about executive salaries. This strengthens the credibility of the evidence.
- KPMG's professional reputation would be damaged if it were found to be making false claims about executive salaries. This strengthens the credibility of the evidence.
- The *Independent Business* is a reputable source of information about issues relating to business and finance. This strengthens the credibility of this document as a source of business-related information.
- The *Independent Business* should have reporters who understand business and access to analysts and consultants who understand business. This therefore strengthens the credibility of this document.

c)
- It is plausible that students who were in a good mood are more likely to believe the claims made by Internet videos about UFOs and ghosts. This is not far-fetched or unlikely. This strengthens the credibility of the claims.
- Laura King has expertise as a psychology professor. This is directly relevant expertise so it makes her claims more credible.
- We would expect someone of King's expertise to conduct an experiment properly, but we do not know enough about the experiment to be sure. This weakens the credibility of the evidence slightly, because we would want to know that the experiment was conducted in controlled conditions.
- *Psychologies* has a reputation for being a good lay psychology magazine with access to the expertise of trained psychologists. This would strengthen the credibility of the document as a source of information about the results of psychology experiments.

5 The credibility criteria

OCR AS Critical Thinking

2.

Elisha's credibility is weakened by her vested interest to say that she has done her homework to avoid getting into more trouble and by her reputation as someone who has previously not done homework.

Darren's claims conflict with Elisha's, which would further weaken the credibility of Elisha's claims if Darren is truthful.

However, Elisha's claims are plausible. It is also plausible that she would get upset about everything going wrong and not being believed if she is trying.

The fact that Elisha flings her memory stick at Mrs Kapoor probably increases the credibility of her claims, as she would be unlikely to do so if her homework were not on it.

Kayeleigh's evidence corroborates Elisha's claims to have tried to print before lessons began and provides a plausible explanation of her lateness that does not conflict with Elisha's claims and thus weakens the credibility of Darren's claims.

Elisha's mother also corroborates her claims, which makes Elisha's claim more credible.

Darren is not particularly credible, as he seems to have a vested interest to get back at Elisha for ditching him, which would be supported by both Mrs Kapoor and Kayleigh. Darren's reputation, as given by Kayleigh, is not good ('She's doing much better without you'), which further weakens his credibility.

Kayleigh appears to be Elisha's friend, which would give her a bias in Elisha's favour. However, this does not weaken the credibility of her claims that much – there's probably not a lot to be gained from sticking up for Elisha at the moment.

Mrs Lewis might be biased in favour of her daughter, which might weaken the credibility of her claims, but the tone of her letter is credible. She does corroborate her daughter's story (and independently, Kayleigh's) and offer explanations that would support Elisha's claims. So, despite her bias, Mrs Lewis is quite credible.

On the whole, it seems as if, on this occasion, Elisha probably did do her homework. All the evidence points towards someone who is trying to sort themselves out, rather than someone who is not trying and lying to cover it.

5.3 Extension

1. EFSA's claim, 'human exposure to bisphenol A (BPA) was well within safety limits and posed no immediate risks to health' contradicts researchers' claims that, 'BPA is present in human tissues at concentrations ten times higher than those considered safe by government agencies'.

2. This is a complex matter that can only be understood by people with a high level of scientific competence. Most of us do not have the expertise to understand the issue well enough to judge. There also seems to be disagreement between scientists and accusations that funding from sources with vested interest may lead to inaccurate results, which make it harder for the non-scientist to judge whether this chemical is currently a threat to our health.

3. EFSA is a government agency. As such, it ought to be neutral because it has no motive to lie and should be interested primarily in people's safety. This would strengthen the credibility of the evidence it provides. It ought to employ scientists with sufficient expertise, which would strengthen its credibility.

   Government agencies are not always neutral, because they are dependent on the government for funding, and governments have agendas. This would weaken the credibility of the EFSA.

   This agency has been accused of having commercial bias – that is, that a vested interest to keep their funding might affect the way they interpret their results in favour of the sponsors. It has not satisfactorily answered that accusation.

4. Vom Saal appears to have a strong reputation and expertise as he is leading an expert panel of 37 international researchers. This increases his credibility.

   We do not know where vom Saal's funding comes from. So he may not be independent and may therefore have a vested interest we do not know about. This weakens his credibility.

   Reviewing 700 scientific papers certainly seems to give the team the ability to perceive what is the case and thus increases the credibility of their claims.

5. Vom Saal's evidence seems more credible, because we know more about his methods. The EFSA's denial seems to be meaningless.

5.1 Foundation

1. **Consider statements a) to e) below. How plausible are they?**

   a) Healing works! Miriam heals through an avatar using the Vibrations of Unconditional Love. (Advert in local organic shop.)

   b) British people buy 198 million items of clothing each year that we later regret.

   c) Shopping online will cost you tens of pounds each month less than visiting the local supermarket.

   d) Use 'Reveal' eye cream. Your skin will look visibly younger.

   e) The world's soil is being eroded at least 20 times as fast as it can regenerate.

2. **Read the advert and answer the questions below.**

   > New **Vege-Crackles** are a revolutionary light-bite. Made by combining high-quality seasoning with super-nutritious snack vegetables which are cooked to create a satisfying crunch followed by an explosion of exquisitely excellent taste. Naturally low in fat*, **Vege-Crackles** help bust bulges. Tasty. Healthy. Full stop.
   >
   > *Snack vegetables naturally absorb less fat during the cooking process. 40% less fat than regular **Crackles**.

   a) How plausible are the claims made in this advert?

   b) How is the credibility of the evidence in this advert affected by the criterion of 'vested interest'?

   c) How is the credibility of the evidence in this advert affected by the criterion of 'consistency'?

   d) Which of the claims in this advert are most credible? Why?

3. **Read the text and answer the questions below.**

   I was not driving my car as it was speeding along the M1 at 121mph. I was at home watching TV. I was on my own. I did not report my car stolen until the following morning because I did not know it had been stolen. (Statement to the police)

   a) Assess the credibility of the speaker.

   b) Do you believe the speaker? Why?

5.2 Core

1. **Assess the credibility of the evidence and its source in texts a) to c) below.**

   a) More than a quarter of Britons identified with *The Royle Family* according to a survey.

   (*The Independent*, Monday, 1 October 2007)

   b) Top bosses are now on 100 times average earnings. According to the latest figures from the accountancy firm KPMG, the typical chief executive of a FTSE 100 company has seen their total pay rise by 12% over the past year to reach over £2.6m.

   (*Independent Business*, Monday, 1 October 2007)

   c) Psychology professor Laura King found that students who were in a good mood were more likely to believe the claims made by Internet videos about UFOs and ghosts. Students who prided themselves on their rationality weren't affected by mood at all.

   (*Psychologies*, October 2007)

2. **Read the text below and assess the credibility of Elisha, Darren, Mrs Kapoor, Mrs Lewis and Kayleigh. Do you think Elisha had done her homework? Why?**

Elisha: I have done my homework but our printer wasn't working and I came in early to print it out but the college system had crashed and I haven't had time to try again.

Mrs Kapoor: Well, at least the dog hasn't eaten it this time, Elisha.

Elisha: It's so not fair. You're so against me. I know I got behind and I'm sorry and I've worked really hard to catch up and everything's going wrong and you don't believe me and I can't cope anymore. (Elisha flings memory stick towards Mrs Kapoor and slams out.)

Darren: I reckon it's her new boyfriend distracting her. Anyway, I saw her racing to first lesson this morning in a state like she was late.

Kayleigh: You're just jealous she ditched you. She's doing much better without you. And she was late because she was trying to print her homework out. I was with her.

Dear Mrs Kapoor,

Could you be a little more understanding of my daughter Elisha? She was very distressed not to be believed by you. Elisha was sitting at the computer until 2am this morning. Our printer is broken. Elisha knows she made a bad start at college. She is trying hard to turn things around. Our home situation and her recent boyfriend troubles have made her a bit moody. She is sorry for walking out.

Mrs Lewis

5.3 Extension

Read the text and answer the questions below.

Just how dangerous is bishpenol A, a chemical found in plastic containers and drinking bottles? Six months ago, the European Food Safety Authority (EFSA) concluded that, despite previous links to breast and prostate cancer and a range of developmental problems, human exposure to bisphenol A (BPA) was well within safety limits and posed no immediate risks to health.

Now, a team of researchers has challenged this idea. It reviewed the same set of data and concluded that BPA is present in human tissues at concentrations ten times higher than those considered safe by government agencies, and that the chemical can have damaging impacts on health at far lower concentrations than previously thought. The expert panel, led by Frederick vom Saal at the University of Missouri-Columbia, included 37 international researchers. They reviewed more than 700 scientific papers on BPA.

The EFSA finding is the result of poor science, says Vom Saal. 'To draw the conclusion that [BPA exposure is within safe limits] you have to ignore the publications showing that there is extensive and continuous exposure of humans to BPA. It is unacceptable to pretend that this has not been demonstrated.'

Vom Saal also believes that BPA poses a health risk at concentrations far below those humans are exposed to, a conclusion again at odds with EFSA's finding. A key reason for this discrepancy may be that EFSA dismissed much of the animal data because humans metabolise BPA more quickly than animals. However, Vom Saal says the animal data is relevant.

Vom Saal now plans to examine the scientific rationale behind the EFSA report to identify whether it could have been biased by commercial interests – an allegation EFSA strongly denies. 'We trust both our scientists and the procedures in place to ensure the impartiality of our advice,' an EFSA spokeswoman said.

(*New Scientist*, 11 August 2007, p. 9)

1. Identify two claims that are contradictory.

2. What makes it difficult to judge who is right in this case?

3. Assess the credibility of the EFSA.

4. Assess the credibility of Frederick vom Saal.

5. Whose evidence is more credible? Why?

6 Assessing credibility of individuals, organisations and documents

CHAPTER OVERVIEW

In this chapter, students will consider the credibility of claims, individuals, evidence and documents in more complex, real-life scenarios. They will consider additional information that might be needed to make a judgement about credibility. They will also learn to make judgements about the relative credibility of sources and the probable course of events in a given scenario.

Credibility, additional information and judgement

Student Book Chapter 6 pages 86–101
Specification pp 11 Section 3.1.2 bullets 3 and 4

This chapter extends the skills taught in Chapter 5. Students should be encouraged to question evidence and its sources more thoroughly, and to provide answers in more detail.

Learning objectives
- Assess the credibility of documents and organisations.
- Explain what other information is needed to decide about the credibility of a document or source.
- Assess how far the use of images and graphical representations weakens or strengthens the claims within a document.
- Compare and contrast the credibility of people or organisations.
- Make informed judgements about which source is most/least credible and the probable course of events in a given scenario.

Common problems
Students do not answer questions in enough detail. For example, they are inclined to write, 'X has a vested interest. Weakens.' It would be better to write: 'X has a vested interest to sensationalise events to attract more readers and sell more newspapers. This makes it less likely that their account is objective and makes it less credible.'

Students answer document questions by referring to individual sources within the document rather than considering the document in itself.

Strategies
Give plenty of exam practice and encourage peer marking.

Model answers for students as fully as possible using the guidance to the worksheet and mark schemes.

Be mean with marks. Critical Thinking examiners give marks for precision, thoroughness and depth of thought.

Show students possible answers that do and do not gain full marks and ask them to explain why.

Suggested activities
Worksheets 6.1, 6.2 and 6.3 can be used as straight credibility practice. However, you may find it useful to work through one or more of the sequences of lessons outlined below. These can help students to set the skills they have learnt during the first unit of this course in context. Worksheets 6.1 and 6.3 contain questions relevant to Section A. This will give students useful additional practice as the exam approaches as well as showing them that, in real life, the skills of sections A and B are related.

Healthy Eating: lesson sequence
Ask students to read Worksheet 6.1. Discuss with students what healthy eating means.

If you have time, you may wish to show students excerpts of Jamie Oliver's TV series *School Dinners*. Elicit comparisons with their own experience. As an alternative you might show excerpts from other cookery programmes – perhaps Nigella Lawson cooking something really fattening, and Hugh

Fearnley-Whittingstall producing and cooking food. Compare this with students' own experiences. Highlight this as anecdotal evidence.

It may be appropriate to ask students to conduct a survey of cooking practices, in which they write their own questions and consider their own sample. They can evaluate each others' in terms of sample size, representativeness, whether the questions are leading, etc. For example: 'Do you ever cook food from fresh ingredients?' vs 'Do you usually cook food from fresh ingredients?'

This work could connect with a college- or school-wide health awareness week. Alternatively, you may wish to link it to the debate on size zero models/obesity. It may be that you need to be aware of students with eating disorders, or to temper the opinions of some of the more judgemental students. There are few topics more intimately bound up with love, self-esteem, identity and self-worth than food, and students can be extremely upset by other students' insensitive comments. But a well-regulated Critical Thinking class, where students are comfortable expressing themselves, can be precisely the forum in which students are able to discuss sensitive issues. This work can be followed with the activities on Worksheet 6.1.

Conspiracy Theory: lesson sequence

Use Worksheet 6.2 to consider conspiracy theories. Ask groups of students to find material on the assassination of JFK, the death of Diana, Princess of Wales, the moon landings, the 9/11 attacks. Ask students to assess the credibility of the documents, the individual sources and the specific claims. Students should also use the skills they acquired in Unit 1 Section 1 (pages 6–63) to consider whether evidence and reasons give logical support to conclusions. Encourage students to write full evaluations of credibility and explain how the criteria affect the credibility of the source. This would also make interesting display work. Follow this with Worksheet 6.2.

Applying the skills to complex material

Worksheet 6.3 goes far beyond the requirements of Unit 1 (and even Unit 4) in terms of difficulty of the concepts. However, one of the main applications of credibility skills in real life is when we try to decide what to believe when we do not have the necessary expertise and understanding to come to a conclusion for ourselves. We then have to use criteria to decide which expert to believe.

You could show students images of Steven Pinker and Philip Lieberman (which can quickly be found through an internet search) and explain that these two men have a difference of opinion about language and thought. You might ask whether we should decide who to believe on the basis of their haircut or their smile. Then revise the credibility criteria and emphasise that they can be used in disputes where we do not fully understand the issues.

It is probably worth doing vocabulary exercises before attempting the activities. Perhaps students could underline and look up words in the article that challenge their understanding. Alternatively, you could give them definitions to match to key words.

Worksheet 6.3 includes some questions on analysis. Again, students should be able to identify some argument components even if they do not follow the argument. This sort of practice may be useful preparation for the exam, just in case students do feel uncertain about the topic chosen for the exam.

Questions 8–10 are largely related to discussions you could have in class, and lines of thought that students might follow. Although Unit 1 tests AO 3 'Development of reasoning' only to a limited extent, it can be very useful for students' development if you start teaching this skill from the beginning. It does not matter if students have only basic thoughts, so long as they are developing and improving them. They also enjoy such discussions, and this can keep them enthusiastic even when they are finding that analysis of argument is difficult, unsettling or even a little dry.

Guidance to worksheet activities

All three worksheets that accompany this chapter should give students a chance to practise their exam skills. They all approach credibility in complex situations from a slightly different angle and in a slightly different format. This should enable students to learn to apply their skills flexibly, which should make them adaptable – whether to real life or to changes in the examination format.

6.1 Core

1. The sample is large, so ought to generate representative results if it is well chosen. We do not know if parents were chosen at random from the database, or whether they were the ones who had most often contributed to discussions.

   Even though the database is claimed to be representative of the nation's families, we do not know that those who answered the questions are representative; it may be that those of us who open jars and buy bread are also those who refuse to answer the questions in that sort of survey.

   So the evidence may not be reliable. It certainly seems implausible.

2. The credibility of the survey is strengthened by the claim that experts say the database is representative.

   The credibility of the survey is weakened by the anonymity of the experts.

   The people who sign up to a website about raising kids may have a vested interest to misrepresent their activities to make themselves look or feel like good parents. For example, if people who bake bread once a year with their children answered that they bake their own bread, it would not be false, but it would give a misleading impression. This possibility weakens the credibility of the website as a source of reliable information.

3. Pat Spungin has some expertise as a child psychologist, but this is not relevant to parent cooking behaviour. So it does not strengthen her credibility on this issue.

   As the founder of the Raising-kids website, she probably has a vested interest to persuade more people to cook healthily for the benefit of their children, which might also weaken her credibility.

4. The school inspectors have access to evidence about school meals and have a vested interest to be objective. This strengthens the credibility of the claim that up to one in four pupils is turning their back on school dinners.

   The newspaper article has quoted only the most extreme figure. This selective quotation indicates a vested interest to sensationalise, which weakens the credibility of the newspaper article as a document.

   The information is also based on only 27 schools, which is a very small sample and may therefore not be representative.

   The claim about healthier lunches and banning burgers is factual and believable.

   The example of the teenager is credible because it comes from a reliable source, but it is not necessarily representative.

   The use of evidence which could be unrepresentative shows some signs of selectivity or bias, which would weaken the credibility of the document.

5. It has to be assumed that the reduction in take up of school dinners is caused by them being healthier/by the lack of chips and burgers, whereas the reduction may be because of the publicity about how unhealthy they are.

6. David Laws has a vested interest to make the facts look bad for the government, as he is an opposition politician. This weakens the credibility of his claims. His claims are also exaggerated, which makes them less credible.

7. Neither claim is entirely credible but b) is more credible than a) because it is plausible and fits with experience rather better. Ofsted is also a better, more objective source of information than the website.

8. Although this is not an extension sheet, this question is intended to stretch the most able students. This level of understanding will not be expected of the weakest students. The two articles certainly represent inconsistent attitudes – that food must be freshly made and healthy, but that we won't eat school dinners because they *are* healthy. It is inconsistent to suppose that 70% of mothers make fresh pasta sauce while up to one in four children in some schools will not eat (and are presumably

supported by their parents in not eating) the new, healthy school dinners. These figures imply that most people are quite extreme and do not account for many of us who occupy ground somewhere between these extremes. However, both of these figures are probably too high – 25% was the maximum drop out found by Ofsted in one school, so is not representative of all. It is most likely that different groups of parents hold these views, so it is not actually inconsistent. Just odd.

6.2 Core

The answers that follow are indicative, possible answers. They are not exhaustive.

1. The credibility of document 1 is weakened by the possible vested interest of the website, www.nessie.co.uk to keep its readers by demonstrating evidence that the Loch Ness Monster (LNM) exists.

   It is also weakened by its own bias in its inclination to believe evidence that shows the existence of the LNM rather than questioning it.

   The credibility of the document is superficially strengthened by the attempt at the end to be objective, but the document does not question that the large object is the LNM, or question the credibility of the sightings/So overall, it is not very credible.

2. We do not know how credible the people reporting these sightings are, as we have little information except their descriptions.

   The willingness of these observers to believe that they were seeing the LNM (fairly implausible claims) might weaken their credibility.

   The details of their sightings showed some inconsistency (require quotation to support), which would weaken the evidence.

3. The credibility of document 2 is strengthened by its appearance in *The Times*, which is a reputable newspaper.

   The credibility of the document is also strengthened by the reputation of the writer as an intelligent journalist. (In non-exam conditions, students would be able to look up references to the author. In the exam, they clearly would not be expected to give an opinion on the credibility of a particular journalist unless the information was given in the resource booklet).

   Linklater makes no attempt to be balanced in his treatment of this issue – he is clear that the evidence all points to the lack of existence of such a beast, and that evidence for its existence is demonstrably fraudulent or mistaken. We can question to what extent this weakens the credibility of the document. In my view, it does not – he is referring to the LNM in a wider context, rather than considering whether it exists on the basis of the evidence to be scrutinised in this piece.

   Furthermore, the language of this piece is rational rather than emotional, the claims are plausible and it is an argument. Arguments, as attempts to persuade, are not balanced.

4. The credibility of Professor Plume is weakened by the fact that he sounds like a character from Cluedo, and bears many hallmarks of being a spoof although he is presented in all seriousness on the website.

   The letters after Professor Plume's name do not appear to relate to any real qualifications, which also weakens his credibility.

   Professor Plume's credibility is seriously weakened by the poor quality of his reasoning; it is inconsistent to maintain that there have been fourteen, 'unique' plesiosaurs. It is terrible reasoning, as we shall see in Unit 2, to assume the conclusion to be true and bend the evidence to fit without questioning it.

   Plume's claims are far-fetched, so not very plausible, which weakens their credibility.

5. The claim is not supported at all. Some evidence is quoted but that's not the same as showing it to be overwhelming.

6. The images in document 1 show that the LNM has been described in many ways, which may or may not be consistent with a single creature – but they are not evidence.

   The image in document 3 is laughable. It is a childlike sketch which cannot be evidence for the existence of a plesiosaur. It therefore has very little use as evidence and no credibility.

6 Assessing credibility of individuals, organisations and documents

7. The image is grainy and unclear. The subject could be an elephant trunk, a plastic monster, an octopus tentacle or almost anything in water so it is not useful.

   There is no idea of scale – to be really useful we would also need a shot with a wider view and supporting evidence to show that the photograph was actually taken when and where the photographer claims it was.

   Photographs could be faked fairly easily even in the 1970s by those with vested interests to do so. So this image at best shows only that there was something in some water somewhere. That is not sufficient to show that the LNM is real.

8. The theory of frozen dinosaur eggs is not very plausible. We do not know for certain that it is impossible, but it seems highly unlikely. Fourteen plesiosaurs in particular is very far fetched. Either two eggs made the unlikely journey through time and hatched at the same time so that they could breed, or fourteen of them did.

9. Document 2 is most credible because it is rational and not trying to force weak evidence to fit a theory. Document 1 is more credible than document 3 because it doesn't make wild claims.

10. It implies that evidence is not important to conspiracists, or that they do not understand the role that evidence can play in forming our beliefs. It implies that a sensational story is more important than a sound one. This question could raise interesting issues in discussion.

11. The following is a suggested answer. Other answers which consider relative credibility, consistency and plausibility in a thoughtful way would also be possible.

    On balance, it is unlikely that the Loch Ness Monster is real. Document 1 has limited credibility regarding the existence of the monster. We can believe its reports of sightings, but the people claiming to have seen the LNM are not very credible. Document 3 is not at all credible because it appears to be a spoof and because it takes the existence of at least 14 unique plesiosaurs for granted. Both of these documents also come from sources which have a vested interest in accepting the existence of the Loch Ness Monster.

    The images are not useful in deciding whether there is a LNM or just a large object, and even the nessie.co.uk website, which would have a vested interest in putting forward the existence of a monster, claims that 'the best that can be said for them is that the majority refer to some large object'.

    There is no corroborating evidence between documents 1 and 3. Both refer to photos and sightings, but many of the images in document 1 are *not* consistent with the description given in document 3.

    Document 2 comes from a neutral source with a reputation for attempting to be objective and a journalist with a strong reputation. It claims that 'every alleged photograph of the monster has been exposed as a demonstrable fraud', which conflicts with the claim in document 3 that 'I don't believe that any of these incredible sightings and reports are fake'. Document 2 also gives us a good reason for continued belief in a monster that has no scientific backing. Furthermore, the claims in document 2 are less far-fetched than the claims in document 3.

6.3 Extension

Section A questions

1. R1: Everyday words like 'fire', 'table' or 'dog' have multiple meanings. R2: The same words can mean different things to different folks. R3: A short session with the *Oxford English Dictionary* confirms that a word's meaning can change over time.

2. 'If meanings could be freely reinterpreted in context, language would be a wet noodle and not up to the job of forcing new ideas into the minds of the listeners.'

3. Books, film, television/fire, table, dog.

4. Studies such as those reported by Alex Martin and Linda Chao (*Current Opinion in Neurobiology*,

OCR AS Critical Thinking 6 Assessing credibility of individuals, organisations and documents

vol 11, p. 194) show that a word activates the same areas of the brain that are involved in perceiving the thing to which the word refers. (This is paraphrase of the conclusions of research.)

5. To highlight its great importance as evidence that should not be ignored.

6. If Pinker's hardwired elementary concepts actually existed, genetic variation would ensure that some people lacked a concept or two. (Strictly speaking the next sentences until 'and so on' are part of this HR.)

Section B questions

1. No. It describes one way of thinking about language and thought, and then writes an argument showing how this is wrong.

2. It weakens the credibility to the extent that it makes it harder for us to know whether to believe Lieberman. On the other hand, this is a perfectly acceptable technique for arguing so it does not really weaken the credibility.

3. The document was published in the *New Scientist*, which is a reputable magazine, and written by a man with relevant expertise. These factors both strengthen the credibility of the document. The claims seem plausible.

4. Stephen Pinker has relevant expertise that strengthens his credibility.

5. Philip Lieberman may have a vested interest to portray his own theories as very much better than those of the person who disagrees with him. Thus he might misrepresent the other theory and make it seem less rational (this is in fact the case – something of a straw person argument, reference Unit 2, Chapter 11, page 190). This would weaken the document's credibility as far as the claims about Pinker's theories go.

6. It is hard to know who is more credible. Both are experts. In the information we have available, Lieberman has justified his argument and provided evidence, which makes him seem more credible. Lieberman's claims also seem more plausible to me.

7. We would need a justification of Pinker's argument rather than just an outline of it. We would need to see his evidence.

8–10.
These are topics for discussion, and you can do as much or as little research on this with your students as you feel is appropriate.

It is useful to students to develop their own ideas, and to challenge their understanding, but these questions go beyond the OCR specification in terms of content.

It may be fairest to Pinker to refer to an extract from his book. You may also wish to suggest to students that Lieberman could be over-simplifying or misrepresenting Pinker's ideas.

Ask students to refer to their own experience. They should have experienced learning some new words during this exercise. Did this feel like 'primal concepts' being lit up? How reliable is such introspection?

A great deal of teenage fantasy and science-fiction plays with the concept of a name as somehow encapsulating the 'essence' of something or someone. In novels such as Ursula LeGuin's *Earthsea Quartet* or Alison Croggon's *Pellinor* series, knowledge of someone's true name gives power over that person. In ancient times, the city of Rome had a secret name (an anagram of *Roma Amor*), which was known only to the Pontifex Maximus, and it was believed that if their enemies ever discovered this name, the city would fall.

Many of us feel somehow identified by our name. Yet language appears to give arbitrary names to objects. Students may be interested in researching statistics about names and life-chances, or names that match our work.

6.1 Core

Read both articles and answer the questions that follow.

Document 1

Modern mothers warm to home cooking

Chicken nuggets, pizza and chips are rapidly falling out of favour with concerned mothers who are spearheading a revival of home cooking, according to research. The majority of mothers are said to prefer to cook meals from scratch rather than open a jar or heat ready meals. Almost three-quarters (70%) of the parents surveyed claimed to make their own pasta sauce; two-thirds said they baked their own bread and the same proportion said that they cooked burgers from scratch. More than two-thirds (68%) baked children's birthday cakes rather than buying them.

The research, conducted by Raising-kids, a parenting website, was based on a poll of more than 2,500 parents from its database, which external experts say is an accurate reflection of the British family population. Pat Spungin, a child psychologist and founder of the website, said that it seemed the days of families sitting down to ready meals were over.

'The proliferation of cookery programmes, the concern about childhood obesity and worries over food additives have pushed food to the top of the parenting agenda,' she said.

The survey found that cooking was as much entertainment as necessity. Seventy per cent of parents said that they cooked or baked for fun with their children, with 52% sitting down to watch cookery programmes as a family. The survey was conducted to mark the Back to the Table Campaign which encourages parents to cook.

(*The Times*, Monday, 1 October, p. 22)

Document 2

Oliver's campaign fails as pupils give up school dinners

The real consequence of Jamie Oliver's media drive for healthy school meals has been to stop children eating at school at all. A report by school inspectors on 27 schools reveals that up to one in four pupils in some schools have turned their back on the new style lunches – which banned burgers and limited the supply of chips. One teenager told inspectors he was getting fitter as a result of regular walks to the chip shop at lunch times.

David Laws, Liberal Democrat Spokesman, said, 'There is no point in having healthy meals if nobody is eating them. The government's worthy aspiration of healthy meals has backfired because of inadequate funding and rushing through changes.'

(*The Independent*, 3 October 2007)

1. How reliable is the evidence from the Raising-kids survey in document 1? (Consider the sample size, etc. from the Student Book Chapter 3, page 43.)

2. How credible is the Raising-kids survey as a source of information?

3. Assess the credibility of Pat Spungin.

(*continued overleaf*)

6.1 Core

(cont.)

4. How credible is the information given in the first paragraph of document 2?

5. What is assumed in the first paragraph of document 2?

6. Assess the credibility of David Laws' claim.

7. Which of the following claims are you more inclined to believe? Why?

    a) The days of families sitting down to ready meals are over.

    b) The real consequence of Jamie Oliver's media drive for healthy school meals has been to stop children eating at school at all.

8. These two documents appeared in the same week in 2007. Are they consistent with each other? Or can only one of them be true?

6.2 Core

Loch Ness Monster: myth or reality?

Document 1. This drawing shows various body shapes sketched by different observers.

Statistics: In 20% of sighting a back or body is reported as distinct from the appearance of humps, and the most common description is that of 'an upturned boat', but others have said: 'It looked like an elephant's back – stood about 4ft high and 10–12ft in length – an egg-shaped body – seen end on there is a distinct angle at apex of back – a long dark body – like a gigantic eel 25ft in length and 5ft in diameter.' Descriptions such as these are not very specific and the best that can be said for them is that the majority refer to some very large object.

(Adapted from www.nessie.co.uk)

Document 2. The lesson, which probably needs to be re-learnt at regular intervals, is that the facts are rarely allowed to interfere with a good story. When, last weekend, *The Times* reported that the legend of the Loch Ness monster might finally have to be buried because sightings of the creature had dropped to a record low, the story circled the globe, eliciting weird explanations of what might have happened. Global warming, inevitably, was blamed for its demise ... That every alleged photograph of the monster has been exposed as a demonstrable fraud has done nothing to undermine its credibility. Besides, an entire tourist industry depends on its existence. It has two other elements that all long-lasting myths require to sustain them – it is not susceptible to final proof and most people would prefer to believe the fiction than to dwell on the fact.

(Magnus Linklater, *The Times*, 3 October 2007)

(*continued overleaf*)

(*cont.*)

Document 3. Loch Ness Zooplankton and Cryogenic Distribution and Deployment Equivalence Theory: Professor Plume PHd MgPollkP GHdiY FghTTR (Loch Ness Research Team Leader), Stuart Pott, Professor Kettle (*et al.*)

I have always taken it for granted that Loch Ness has been home to at least fourteen unique plesiosaurs since the Ice Age and I believe that a good deal of evidence exists to support this contention.

For example, so many witnesses have seen plesiosaur-like forms both in and around the loch: the Spicer sighting; the eerie Spokker-Jackson sighting; and the famous Surgeon's photo all clearly seem to show a plesiosaur-like head and neck. I don't believe that any of these incredible sightings and reports are fakes and would challenge anyone to prove such a thing. Indeed, taken together the evidence is quite overwhelming and goes a long way to explain the enduring legend of sea-horses, serpents and beasts in Loch Ness. The scientific task for my Loch Ness research project is therefore not to prove that a monster, Nessie, lives unseen in Loch Ness, but rather to establish the mechanism whereby she managed to reach the loch and to survive with her peers 350 million years after the rest of her kind went extinct. This is perhaps the most incredible story of scientific discovery since Darwin.

It is easy to see how dinosaur eggs (s.155/3) could have been trapped under the seismically disturbed crust that formed Pangea. Here they would quickly freeze to temperatures well below minus 150°C and, as my new laboratory has demonstrated, survive for up to 350 millon years. Hundreds of millions of years ago Pangea broke up into some of the continents we see today. I am convinced that the frozen dinosaur eggs survived and were carried by the shifting land masses until they reached the area now known as Loch Ness. As the Ice Age melted away, the ancient but preserved living material within the eggs thawed and hatched into first generation Loch Ness Monsters. This took place approximately 10,000 years ago and their successors have lived in the deep dark loch ever since. They may be our only direct link to a long-extinct past.

(www.lochness.co.uk/exhibition/lochness-cryogenic.html)

1. Assess the credibility of document 1.

2. Document 1 refers to statistics taken from a number of individual sightings of the Loch Ness Monster. How credible are these individual sightings? (*continued overleaf*)

6.2 Core

(cont.)

3. Assess the credibility of document 2.

4. Assess the credibility of Professor Plume (document 3).

5. 'The evidence is quite overwhelming.' How well supported is this claim in document 3?

6. How useful are the images in documents 1 and 3 as evidence?

7. How useful is the image below, taken from Urquhart castle, as evidence of the existence of the Loch Ness Monster?

A picture of the alleged Loch Ness monster taken from Urquhart Castle on 21 May 1977 (Fortean Picture Library).

(www.unexplainedstuff.com/Mysterious-Creatures/Monsters-of-Land-Sea-and-Air.html)

8. How plausible is the theory of frozen dinosaur eggs (document 3)?

9. Which document is the most credible? Why?

10. What does the cartoon below imply about the way conspiracy theorists use evidence?

(www.cartoonstock.com/directory/l/loch_ness_monster.asp)

11. How likely is it that the Loch Ness Monster is real? Justify your judgement.

6.3 Extension

Read the article and answer the questions on the next page.

'Stand up for the wet noodles' by Philip Lieberman

Steven Pinker* starts from the idea that language and grammar are hardwired into our brains. Like Chomsky, he believes that the rules of grammar for every language on Earth lie dormant in children's brains, like software that has been preloaded into our brain's hard drive by evolution.

In *The Stuff of Thought* Pinker extends this idea from grammar to words themselves. According to Pinker, we don't learn the meanings of particular words, but instead have a store of 'primal concepts' that are activated when we hear a word. These concepts – such as cause, motion, space and time – comprise the elementary building blocks of language and thought. Presumably when a child sees her mother point to a dog and hears her say 'dog', innate primal concepts like animate, animal, safe and perhaps edible are activated. Innate concepts, says Pinker, give language its power. 'If meanings could be freely reinterpreted in context, language would be a wet noodle and not up to the job of forcing new ideas into the minds of the listeners.'

To me it seems clear that we actually learn the meanings of most words through experience, or through secondary sources such as books, film and television. Everyday words like 'fire', 'table' or 'dog' have multiple meanings, and the same words can mean different things to different folks. A short session with the *Oxford English Dictionary* confirms that a word's meaning can change over time.

The 10-tonne gorillas missing from *The Stuff of Thought* are neurophysiological studies showing how the brain deals with words and their meanings. Studies such as those reported by Alex Martin and Linda Chao (*Current Opinion in Neurobiology*, vol 11, p194) show that a word activates the same areas of the brain that are involved in perceiving the thing to which the word refers. (So hearing the word 'dog' activates the same bit of your brain that you use when you see or hear a dog.)

Ultimately, Pinker neglects the single biological truth that rules out innate detailed knowledge of language: genetic variation. If Pinker's hardwired elementary concepts actually existed, genetic variation would ensure that some people lacked a concept or two. We would encounter people who could not acquire the meanings of entire sets of words, or think or act on these concepts. A child missing the gene coding for the primal concept kinship would never be able to understand words such as 'family', 'cousin', 'mother' and so on. Certainly humans possess an innate capacity to acquire language, but genetic variation rules out theories that posit innate knowledge of language's details.

(*New Scientist,* 3 October 2007, issue 2624)

Philip Lieberman is the Fred M. Seed Professor of Cognitive and Linguistic Sciences at Brown University in Providence, Rhode Island.

* Stephen Pinker is the Johnstone Family Professor in the Department of Psychology at Harvard University. Until 2003 he taught in the Department of Brain and Cognitive Sciences at MIT.

6.3 Extension

Section A Questions

1. Identify three reasons to support Lieberman's claim that, 'we actually learn the meanings of most words through experience, or through secondary sources such as books, film and television'.

2. Identify the hypothetical reasoning in paragraph 2.

3. Identify the examples used in paragraph 3.

4. Identify the evidence in paragraph 4.

5. Why does Lieberman call this evidence a '10-tonne gorilla'?

6. Identify the hypothetical reasoning in paragraph 5.

Section B Questions

1. Does the document 'Stand up for the wet noodles' give fair coverage to both sides of this dispute?

2. How does this affect its credibility?

3. Assess the credibility of the document (using other criteria than balanced coverage).

4. Assess the credibility of Stephen Pinker.

5. Assess the credibility of Philip Lieberman.

6. Who is more credible? Justify your answer.

7. What additional evidence would you need to make a judgement about whose theories were right – Pinker's or Lieberman's?

General Discussion

8. Do you think we learn words and grammar through experience or that we are born with primal concepts?

9. Can we have ideas that we don't have the words for?

10. Does a name express something's essence?

UNIT 1 — Guidance to the Activities

ACTIVITY 1

Look back at the Key Terms definitions of 'conclusion' and 'reason'. Identify the reason(s) and conclusion in each of the following arguments.

A (reason) You enjoy dealing with different people. (conclusion) You should look for a career that involves dealing with people.

B (reason) The bus service on this route is useless. (conclusion) We ought to complain to the bus company.

C (reason) We are short of money this week. (reason) Beans on toast is cheap. (conclusion) We had better have beans on toast for tea today.

D (reason) The sun is very strong today and (reason) you are going to lie on the beach. (conclusion) You should put on plenty of sun cream.

E (reason) Heavy snow is forecast later on. (reason) The police have advised everyone to stay at home. (conclusion) You should stay home and not go to work.

F (reason) You are allergic to dog hair. (reason) The friends you are going to visit have a dog. (conclusion) You ought to take some medication to reduce your allergic reaction.

ACTIVITY 3

Decide whether each of the following is an argument or not. if it is an argument, identify the conclusion and the reason(s). Explain your answer.

A (not an argument)

B (argument)

   (reason) Other ways of punishing criminals are less effective than locking them up.

   (conclusion) The government should spend more on building new prisons.

C (not an argument)

D (argument)

   (reason) I want to go on holiday after my exams.

   (reason) I find being by the sea is very relaxing.

   (conclusion) I ought to book a holiday at the seaside.

E (not an argument)

F (not an argument)

G (not an argument)

Unit 1 Guidance to the Activities · OCR AS Critical Thinking

ACTIVITY 4

For each of the passages below, state whether it is an argument or not. If it is an argument add *one* more reason in support of the conclusion.

A **(not an argument)**

B **(argument)**

C **(argument)**

D **(argument)**

E **(not an argument)**

ACTIVITY 5

a) Identify the argument indicator words in this passage. State whether they indicate a reason or the conclusion.

We should **(conclusion indicator)** all try to recycle more of our kitchen waste, since **(reason indicator)** this would reduce the amount of waste taken to landfill sites, and also because **(reason indicator)** kitchen waste can be turned into useful compost.

b) Arguments A–C below do not include argument indicators. Rewrite them with the words 'because' or 'therefore' in the right place to help show the reasons and the conclusion.

A Because you can read during the journey and
because you do not need to worry about breakdowns or traffic jams,
therefore trains are a better way to travel than a car.

B Because many games end 0–0 and
because results matter only for the teams at the top or bottom of a table,
therefore football is not as exciting as commentators suggest.

C Because the most popular meal in the UK is now chicken tikka masala and
because spaghetti bolognese has replaced sausages and mash as a staple family meal,
therefore we should re-think our view of what constitutes classic British food.

c) Look back at the arguments in Activity 1 (page 8). Insert suitable argument indicator words in each to show the reason(s) and conclusions. Other answers may be correct.

A **(reason)** Because you enjoy dealing with different people, **(conclusion)** therefore **(conclusion indicator)** you should **(already a conclusion indicator)** look for a career that involves dealing with people.

B **(reason)** Since the bus service on this route is useless, **(conclusion)** therefore we ought to complain to the bus company.

C **(reason)** Because we are short of money this week and **(reason)** since beans on toast is cheap, **(conclusion)** it follows that we had better have beans on toast for tea today.

D **(reason)** Since the sun is very strong today and **(reason)** as you are going to lie on the beach, **(conclusion)** it follows that you should put on plenty of sun cream.

E **(reason)** As heavy snow is forecast later on and **(reason)** because the police have advised everyone to stay at home **(conclusion)** consequently you should stay home and not go to work.

OCR AS Critical Thinking   Unit 1 Guidance to the Activities

F   **(reason)** Because you are allergic to dog hair and **(reason)** as the friends you are going to visit have a dog, **(conclusion)** it follows that you ought to take some medication to reduce your allergic reaction.

ACTIVITY 6

In each of the following arguments, there are two reasons and a conclusion. Identify these three elements using the appropriate notation.

A
R1 Gas is an inexpensive way to heat your home.
R2 Gas heating boilers are small and neat.
C   You should install gas central heating to heat your home.

B
R1 Spending long periods in front of a computer screen can cause eye strain.
R2 You've been working on the computer for several hours.
C   You should have a break from the computer.

C
R1 Hair dye can ruin the condition of hair.
R2 You have had your hair dyed several times recently.
C   You would be wise to use conditioner to improve the condition of your hair.

D
R1 We need a new television.
R2 Pentang televisions have the latest technology.
C   We ought to buy a Pentang.

E
R1 The company has gained extra business in the last six months.
R2 People with up-to-date IT skills will be needed to help develop the new computer system.
C   The company should recruit young people who have just left college.

F
R1 The same old work and study routine gets very boring.
R2 Lack of exercise is making you feel unhealthy.
C   You should try Soaks, the new and different fitness centre.

G
R1 The government's campaign to get us to eat more healthily is doomed to fail to reduce obesity.
R2 Increasing exercise and reducing calorie intake work in very few cases.
C   The government should direct money towards researching the causes of obesity instead.

ACTIVITY 7

Identify the counter-argument or counter-assertion in the following arguments.

A   It is commonly taken for granted that the introduction of GM crops should be strictly regulated. **(counter-assertion)** Opponents claim that they will be unsafe for human consumption and take over the countryside. **(counter-assertion)**

B   Supposedly, the smoking ban was going to protect the health of workers and customers. **(counter-assertion)**

C Officials argue that people are using the library service less because nowadays cut-price books can be bought in supermarkets. **(counter-argument comprising reason and conclusion)**

ACTIVITY 8

A Children don't get enough exercise. **(claim)**

B I intend to visit France this summer, even if I can only afford it by stopping going out with friends. **(claim expressing intention to do something)**

C If you visit France, you will find the way of life is far more relaxed than in this country. **(hypothetical claim)**

D You ought to go to Professor Bloxwich's lecture, provided you have nothing else planned for today. **(hypothetical claim which could be worded:** 'If you have nothing else planned for today, then you ought to go to Professor Bloxwich's lecture.'**)**

ACTIVITY 9

The hypothetical reasoning from the passages is as follows.

A If the government seriously wants to cut crime, then it should impose a curfew on know criminals every 28 days when the moon is full.

B If this is the case, then it explains why I'm always kept waiting 15 minutes before my call is answered by a bored operative: (I live in an area with the wrong postcode).

C It will happen if Argentina keeps winning.

ACTIVITY 10

Following are the assumptions.

A The writer must assume: that a car is the only way that Raj can transport his drum kit to gigs and that he will not need car transport for a guitar; that the band needs a guitarist.

B The writer must assume: that the normal bus will not arrive on time in the current traffic conditions; that the earlier bus is early enough to allow for the increased traffic and will arrive on time.

ACTIVITY 12

A is not in the passage, but it is not an assumption. The argument is that some scientists have gone abroad, but not that the best of them have.

B is not in the passage, but it is not an assumption. The argument is about stopping the brain drain not about bringing scientists back to Britain.

D is not in the passage, but it is not an assumption. The argument is about scientists, so it really does not matter for this argument if other professionals were attracted abroad.

The writer does need to assume C. The writer is arguing that injecting money into the situation will prevent the brain drain. For this to solve the problem, it must be assumed that it was financial factors that led to the brain drain in the first place. C expresses this assumption.

OCR AS Critical Thinking Unit 1 Guidance to the Activities

ACTIVITY 13

Following are possible answers.

A   The author assumes that in a significant percentage (or a significant proportion) of cases the act of giving up smoking will lead to the ex-smoker having fewer smoking-related illnesses that put a strain on the health service.

B   The author assumes that most children (**not** all children) have access to a library with a specialist adviser.

C   The author assumes that rules and tactics are the only aspects of rugby or football that make them exciting.

ACTIVITY 14

A
Conclusion: We may be unwise in trying to eradicate hookworm infections in these countries.
Possible assumption: Most people in poor countries have only mild hookworm infections that do not cause diarrhoea.

B
Conclusion: We might be wise to base our approach to dreams on the science of the brain rather than fashion.
Possible assumption: Analysing dreams may interfere with the processes that remove useless information from our brains.

C
Conclusion: Maybe we should all start hoping our national teams lose big matches (as this is bound to reduce the amount of violence surrounding the matches).
Possible assumption: Fans are likely to drink even more alcohol when they are in a good mood.

ACTIVITY 15

Evidence: Research carried out by the University of Hertfordshire involving interviewing 100 people aged between 22 and 45 who had been speed-dating.

Examples: 'I have a PhD in computing' and 'What is your favourite pizza topping?'

ACTIVITY 16

The forms of evidence are as follows.

A   (A survey reveals that) while 40% of teenagers have no religious faith, the level of unbelievers drops to a mere 8% in the over-65 age group. **(accept estimate for 40% and accept numerical data or statistical data)**

B   (Research shows) there are currently 530 million unused coat hangers stored in UK homes. This would equate to 17,000 tonnes of plastic **(numerical and statistical data)**; customers can bring unwanted hangers into stores on the days of the amnesty and place them in the recycling boxes. **(factual claim)**

C   More than 3.5 million people in Britain – 6% of the population – belong to a gym or fitness club **(numerical and statistical data)**; growing numbers of scientists accept that punishing workouts are unnatural **(factual claim)**; Jim Fixx, the American pioneer of jogging, collapsed and died at the age of 52 **(example)**.

D   The increase in numbers of a wild bird in Scotland despite its declining numbers in the rest of Europe has mystified experts **(factual claim)**; RSPB Scotland said it was delighted but it was a mystery as to why red-throated divers had done so well **(statement from a source)**; their numbers have risen from 935 to 1255 breeding pairs in twelve years **(numerical data)**; in Shetland the population has dropped from 700 pairs to 407 **(numerical data)**; Dr Mark Eaton, an RSPB scientist, said: 'We feared the numbers of red-throated divers might drop because the warming of the North Sea seems to be reducing stocks of the fish they feed on.' **(statement from a source)**

ACTIVITY 17

In the examination responses would not be expected to be as lengthy as those given below. Answers could include the following or other relevant evaluation.

a)
- A We need more information about how the survey was conducted to be sure that the evidence is reliable: how many people were asked? Who was asked – people who visit National Trust sites, or visit their website? Older people who remember the white cliffs of Dover as the first view of home after a trip abroad? People who live in Kent? In any case, 22% does not constitute a majority, so this evidence does not support the claim that the white cliffs of Dover were 'runaway winners'.

- B The survey of 23 men is insufficient to give reliable evidence to support the claim that using Phwoire combats signs of ageing. The percentages merely give figures for men who agree with claims, which is not really evidence to support the claims, as there is no objective measure of the wrinkliness of the users. We would need to know how the survey was conducted: was it by means of simple yes/no questions, or something more structured? Who conducted it – Phwoire marketing staff or independent scientists?

b)
- A We have no information as to the questions that were asked, for example what was meant by 'no religious faith', which might include 'don't knows'/agnostics, or might mean everyone who does not regularly attend religious worship, but does have some belief. We have no information about the size of the survey, so we do not know if the sample was representative of all teenagers or of all people over the age of 65. People over the age of 65 covers a very wide range – could be people over 100, or people who are only just over 65, who very likely would not see themselves as close to death/the Pearly Gates (since their life expectancy is probably another 20 years).

- B The research methodology and the sample surveyed are not given, so we have no way of knowing how reliable the survey was. If it was carried out with customers in one particular Marks & Spencer shop, or just a small number of people, they might be wealthier than average, have more clothes, and therefore retain a higher number of coat hangers.

    The research shows there are 530 million unused coat hangers in UK homes, which is about 8 or 9 unused coat hangers per person (based on a population of 60 million). This could be seen as not very many when compared with the number of clothes that the average person has in their wardrobe (101 items according to Oxfam's research, but answers are not expected to be that specific). The figure is average, meaning that some people have many more and some people very few.

Responses could also suggest that holding on to a few coat hangers is not necessarily wasteful of recyclable plastic, because plastic coat hangers break easily, and because plastic coat hangers come in different types and sizes (for different clothes). The quantity of plastic given in tonnes appears very large, but is a very small amount per household/per person.

C   The survey might be misleading if the people questioned were within a particular age group, or income bracket, and therefore more likely to have the money to join a club than the population as a whole. Many of them may be members as much for social reasons as because they wish to be involved in 'punishing' physical activity. It is likely that not all the people who belong to a gym or fitness club use it regularly – many people join a gym after Christmas, for example, but after the first few weeks revert to their normal, less active lifestyle.

The majority of members of gyms or fitness clubs are not necessarily engaging in the type of punishing workout which is ultimately damaging. The example of Jim Fixx is not necessarily relevant; we do not have information about the condition which killed him, but he might have died younger if he had not engaged in physical activity, or his collapse might have been completely unaffected by his jogging.

D   The increase recorded in red-throated divers in one part of Scotland is 320 pairs over 12 years or just two or three pairs each year, and the decrease in Shetland is of a similar order – a very small percentage each year. We do not know how accurate these figures are – can the scientists really be sure they have counted every bird in the red diver population?

ACTIVITY 18

Possible answers are given below. Other responses may be reasonable.

The evidence gives an increase in rubbish recycled or composted from 30% to 34% in 2006/7. We don't know how this was measured (weight or volume), or whether the total amount of rubbish has increased or decreased. If the total amount of rubbish is less, but the amount recycled is a higher percentage, it may be that the recycled rubbish is actually less, not more.

The writer claims that, 'it means more of you are recycling', but the evidence does not support this. It may be that the same people are recycling more rubbish. The writer also claims, 'more recyclable bits and pieces are being put to good use'. However, even though people are putting more rubbish into the recycling system, that does not necessarily mean it is then put to good use.

The article claims that an Audit Commission survey showed that litter was at a very low level in the borough, making it one of the cleanest places in the country. We have no information as to how the survey was carried out: did the people carrying out the survey visit different parts of the borough, or just one or two, which were unusually litter-free rather than representative of the borough as a whole. As the Audit Commission is a government body, we may consider that the survey was probably conducted reliably and so the evidence would give support to the claim about the cleanliness of the borough.

There is a jump from 'litter' at a low level to 'clean' in the claim. If we accept these as meaning the same, then the evidence does give some support to the claim.

ACTIVITY 19

a) (For the sake of road safety,) speed cameras should be removed.
b) Counter-argument.
c) Excessive speed is found to be a contributory cause in only 10% of accidents.

Unit 1 Guidance to the Activities OCR AS Critical Thinking

d) Speed cameras do not (even) lead to a reduction in road deaths.
e) The author must assume the following.
- The number of speed cameras has stayed the same over the period.
- Traffic volume/number or length of journeys has not increased over the period.
- The number of people caught is proportional to the number of people who are speeding.

Other assumptions may be correctly identified.

ACTIVITY 20

Either argument notation, or a diagram, or writing out the structure would be acceptable approaches.

Ev1 Researchers combined hospital admission numbers with sport participation figures across the USA in the 1990s. They found for every 10,000 participants overall neck injuries in 5.85 football players,
Ev2 That's more than (2.8) hockey players and (1.67) soccer players combined.
R American football is the sport most likely to cause neck injury in the USA.
C Students concerned for their long-term health should avoid American football.

ACTIVITY 21

a) F1 drivers must surely count amongst the elite of multitaskers.
b) Driving skill is an essential quality in an F1 driver.
 F1 drivers have to be among the very fittest athletes in the world.
 Drivers need to be competent engineers as well.
 The right mental approach is critical.
 Drivers have to perform all these amazing feats at the same time at 200 mph.
c) A typical F1 race can last an hour and a half.
 (In the example about Jensen Button): neck muscles support a weight equivalent to 30 bags of sugar.
d) Jensen Button.

ACTIVITY 22

a)
C Medical science has made little contribution to the health improvement (increased life expectancy and better health) of people in western societies during the last 150 years.
R1 Medical science had little to do with the drop in infant mortality.
R2 The main factor in improvements in life expectancy and health was the action to improve the living conditions of the poor.
R3 Advances in surgical techniques in recent years have not resulted in the dramatic improvements in life expectancy that resulted from late nineteenth century public health improvements.
CA (There is a widespread belief that) medical science has been responsible for the increased life expectancy and better health of people in western societies during the last 150 years.

b)
Ev Figures from Chicago show that the key decline in infant mortality rates in Chicago was between 1870 and 1900. These improvements were due to better sanitation and water supply. The vast majority of the population could not afford to visit the doctor. In Britain vaccination programmes became widespread only in the middle of the twentieth century long after key improvements in life expectancy and health had been achieved.

© Pearson Education Limited 2008

Examples. The chance of reaching the age of 5 increased from 50% to 75% in this period.

Accept as evidence or as example: In Chicago infant mortality fell by 122 per 1000 between 1890 and 1920, but by only 7 per 1000 between 1960 and 1990.

c) The author uses evidence and examples from Chicago which may not be relevant to a wider argument about improvements in health and life expectancy.

ACTIVITY 23

a) Our concept of the age when people retire from work should be revised.

b) Reasons: People are living longer and longer lives.
The birth rate is decreasing and this will result in a significant age imbalance in the population.
The concept of an age when one should 'retire' is a recent one.
Pensions experts have warned that, unless the retirement age is raised, the level of pensions must be reduced.

c) Figures from the 1921 UK census show that 53% of men in the age group 70–74 were still working in spite of pensions being available at the age of 70.

d) Accept answers which argue either for or against the identified assumption being reasonable.

The author must assume that pensions paid to these men were high enough to enable them not to work unless they wished. The passage says they 'chose' to work, but if they could not live on their pension, they had no choice. The assumption is not reasonable.

The author must assume that these men were all receiving a pension. The passage refers to pensions being 'available' at the age of 70, but that does not mean all men in this age group could receive one. The assumption is not reasonable.

e) If you are biologically young (then) you should still be working.

ACTIVITY 24

The quotations are intended to stimulate discussion of whether or not they are reasonable, rather than produce definitive answers. It is likely that B (and possibly F) will be considered implausible.

ACTIVITY 25

a) There is not one right answer to these activities, but answers could include some of the points given below.

B   There is no evidence to support the claim that 'waists are back: this season's essential fashion item is a wide belt', and it seems to be a personal observation. However, it is reasonable since fashion is subject to constant change.

Alternative answers might argue that fashion is very individualistic and the trends which fashion pundits forecast don't always catch on as street fashion; or that wide belts were this season's item, and are therefore now on the way out.

C   The claim that there is no real health hazard in drinking several cups of coffee could be seen as reasonable, since it is supported by the evidence about long-term coffee drinkers and dementia.

However, this evidence does not consider other health hazards which drinking coffee might cause. Dementia alone is not a sufficient measure of health in old age.

We need to know more about how the research was conducted, and its reliability, to establish whether the link between drinking coffee and dementia was related to the coffee itself, or to some other factor such as the lifestyle of the coffee drinkers – perhaps the coffee drinkers keep dementia at bay because they generally lead busy, active lives or have a healthy diet.

D   This claim is reasonable. The claim itself is quite limited – just that 43% of divorced people will have another partner within five years, not that they will re-marry, or even that they will form a permanent relationship with the new partner. The relationship with the new partner may turn out to be very short-lived, but five years is quite a long time period in which to look for a new partner.

It would help in deciding how far the claim is reasonable if we knew how the figures had been arrived at, and what is meant by 'have a new partner'.

E   The claim that channelling white light into buildings will bring them back into balance and harmony is not reasonable. 'Balance' and 'harmony' are meaningless/undefined terms. 'White light' and 'negative energies' sound scientific, but there is no explanation of what they mean. There is no evidence to support the claim.

F   The claim seems to have some information missing – the time period when the aerosols are used. The claim is reasonable if the time period is a year, but less so if it is a short period such as a week or a month. To make a definite judgement we also need to know how the 'average' number of aerosols has been established. What is the average number of people in a 'household' in the survey sample? In some areas this could be a lot of people, in other places, just one or two. Is usage based on use by individuals or does it include aerosols used by people in carrying out their work? It would also help to know what is meant by 'aerosols for food'.

b) Answers could include the following:

A   The claim could be supported, or undermined, by detailed information about the qualifications teachers hold, or their other relevant training, which prepared them to teach the subject, taken since their degree, and evidence about the age of pupils which the teachers are teaching (infant/primary or year 13 for example)?

B   The headline implies that the numbers of children having school lunches have fallen as a result of Jamie Oliver's influence on the content of school lunches. Evidence (supporting) would include information which showed whether this fall is in percentage terms (and how great a percentage), or (undermining) whether it is due to a drop in the overall numbers of school children, whether it is just a short-term fall, which has been reversed, or long term, and whether there were any other factors such as an increase in the cost of school lunches.

C   Evidence about which bugs and which aspect of bugs' behaviour can be used to predict the weather would help support the claim, together with information about how the usefulness of bugs was measured, whether this is a general characteristic of bugs, or something that applies only in certain situations, for example just before rainfall, and how the comparison with normal weather forecasters was made.

D   Evidence about who carried out any research, and how the research programme was constructed might support the claim. Evidence that the research was financed by a pumpkin marketing company might undermine it.

ACTIVITY 26

a)

    A   Witnesses could be under the influence of alcohol (or illegal substances). Lack of visibility due to combination of dark and lighting effects. Witnesses could have been distracted by all the people moving about.

    B   Some elderly people could be confused and their memories unreliable due to medical conditions, prescription medicines, or the influence of alcohol. There could be distractions if there is entertainment or singing taking place.

    C   Poor visibility due to fog. Drivers concentrating on the road ahead, for example, might miss other things happening some distance away.

    D   Emotions running high could affect perception. People could be distracted because there are a lot of people moving about and shouting slogans.

b) The woman's account is weakened by the criterion ability to perceive, because it is likely to have been dark when she was driving home after an evening out and visibility could have been poor. Her perception of what was happening could have been affected if alcohol was part of the evening out.

c) William Blake's evidence is weakened by the criterion ability to perceive as he did not actually inspect the brakes, but formed his opinion on the basis of what his cousin had said. His claim is therefore less reliable than if he had either tested them by driving the car, or actually inspected them.

ACTIVITY 27

Where witnesses' evidence is corroborated:

Senior consumer protection officer stated, 'Both [cars] showed serious faults within days of purchase'. This is corroborated in respect of the car Ethel Blake bought, since the vehicle safety engineer said 'My inspection showed that the car ... had dangerously faulty brakes, which would soon have failed completely'. This would also confirm Atkins' statement that the car had not been properly serviced before it was sold, as this type of fault would have been repaired during a service, and by his plea of guilty to selling a car in an unsafe condition.

ACTIVITY 28

Evidence from sources other than Atkins is brief, but consistent.

Inconsistencies:
Atkins' evidence is inconsistent – he pleaded guilty to two specimen charges of selling a car in an unsafe condition and acknowledged that it had not been properly serviced before Ethel Blake collected it, but this is inconsistent with his denial that the brakes were dangerous, and with his asking the court to take sixteen other offences into consideration.

ACTIVITY 29

a) People whose evidence may be weakened by bias:

    William Blake may be biased towards his cousin Ethel Blake (and vice versa).

Atkins' business partner Colin Davis may be biased in his favour.

Atkins' solicitor, Catherine Lee, has a responsibility to act correctly in her professional role, but is acting for him and may be biased in his favour.

The senior consumer protection officer, Suzy Thomson and the vehicle safety engineer, Tim Harris, should also act neutrally as professionals, but might have been influenced by the complaints received to be biased towards the customers.

b) There are a number of possible sources of unconscious bias which could be identified, for example:

  A Depending on previous relations with her next-door neighbours, Doreen Henderson might be biased towards or against Louise Long. She could be influenced by pre-conceptions about students being, for example, lazy, noisy troublemakers, or think that they would be law-abiding because they attend a good school. She might be biased in favour of Mohammed Hussain and his friends because they do a job which involves hard work. Equally she might have a cultural prejudice against them. She might assume that girls are well-behaved and young men are not (or vice versa).

  B Annabel Waterworth could be prejudiced against Patrick O'Flanaghan for religious or cultural reasons (the name suggests he is of Irish origin), or because he is a trade unionist. She might believe that a member of staff who has resigned no longer supports her employer's interests.

ACTIVITY 30

a) The people who should be neutral are the magistrate, Gurvinder Gosal, the senior consumer protection officer, Suzy Thomson and the vehicle safety engineer, Tim Harris. For all of these it is an expectation of the profession they work in that they act neutrally, and it could damage their career or professional reputation if they were found to have done otherwise.

b) A number of answers are acceptable here, but could include: police officers, forensic scientists, teachers, medical and other researchers, tax and social security workers.

ACTIVITY 31

In each case the vested interest tends to weaken the claims made.

- Ethel Blake has a vested interest in seeing Atkins convicted and getting compensation.
- Atkins has a vested interest in avoiding prison/large fines or other punishment.
- Atkins and Colin Davis both have a vested interest in avoiding damage to Atkins' reputation, and that of their business.
- The senior consumer protection officer, Suzy Thomson, and the vehicle safety engineer, Tim Harris, both have a vested interest in the outcome of the case confirming their professional judgements about Atkins' business practices and the car that was sold.
- The solicitor, Catherine Lee, has a vested interest in being successful as a solicitor and therefore in presenting a good case on Atkins' behalf.

ACTIVITY 32

a)

  A The former athlete has expertise in his sport. Expertise in diet and nutrition would be relevant. The former athlete's expertise is not relevant in this case.

OCR AS Critical Thinking　　　　　　　　　　　　　　　　Unit 1 Guidance to the Activities

　　B　The local police force has expertise in local road conditions and probably has knowledge of which areas have flooded previously. Expertise in both would be needed and the police force's expertise would be relevant in this case.

　　C　The plumber's expertise is likely to be in plumbing, not house electrics and would therefore not be relevant.

　　D　The politician has expertise in politics and law. In this case expertise in business and economics is needed. The politician's expertise is not relevant (unless he has access to government information about the economy).

b)　Sources with specialist expertise:

- William Blake – expertise as car mechanic, relevant to his claim that he knew the brakes were faulty.
- Atkins and Colin Davis – expertise in cars. Atkins' expertise is relevant to the claims made about the car; Davis's is not relevant to his claims about Atkins' character.
- The vehicle safety engineer, Tim Harris – also expertise in cars which is relevant to his evidence that the car's brakes were dangerously faulty.
- Gurvinder Gosal, magistrate – expertise in the law – relevant to his decision.
- The senior consumer protection officer, Suzy Thomson – expertise in consumer law – relevant to the claim that customers bought cars in good faith.
- Catherine Lee, solicitor - expertise in the law – relevant to claim that Atkins had no previous convictions.

ACTIVITY 33

Answers may include some of the following points.

Atkins' reputation is for his charity work for the Retired Greyhounds Rehoming Centre. The effect of this information is at best to slightly strengthen his credibility. It shows he has concerns about dogs, and is prepared to give his time up to carry out charity work for them, but this is not relevant to his expertise with cars, or his honesty as a car dealer.

His reputation as a car dealer also appears to be neutral: we know only that he had no previous convictions, but this shows only that he had never before been found guilty of any charge. The evidence from Atkins' business partner about this previous good character is tained by bias and vested interest, and does not confirm that his reputation was as someone of good character.

Alternatively, answers which argue the impact of these facts on his credibility is neutral would be accepted.

ACTIVITY 36

There is no one right answer to these questions. Answers may argue either way. The claims are likely to be thought credible, apart from B, F and (possibly) G. Answers may cover some of the points below, but should refer to credibility criteria.

　　A　If the scientist has relevant expertise, this would strengthen this claim's credibility.

　　B　Aliens R Us website does not sound like a serious organisation, but rather enthusiastic amateurs. They are likely to be biased towards the belief that aliens exist and take an interest in earthlings. (Answers could also argue they have expertise in this field.)

C   *The Guardian* has a reputation as a newspaper which reports accurately and they quote an organisation with relevant expertise in economic affairs, and a vested interest in maintaining a reputation for accuracy.

D   The information is from a government department which has a vested interest in maintaining its reputation for accuracy.

E   David Attenborough has expertise as an environmentalist and a scientist, plus a reputation as broadcaster on the natural world, which strengthens the credibility of the claim.

F   The supporter is likely to be biased in his club's favour which weakens the credibility of the claim.

G   In this instance the scientist has considerable expertise in this field, and the claim is credible.

ACTIVITY 37

Answers may include some of the following points.

a) As a former politician, Michael Portillo would have expertise to understand the issues which concern voters and this strengthens his credibility. It is also strengthened because he would have a reputation to maintain as he has continued his career in public life, by writing and broadcasting on topical matters. However his credibility may be weakened because, as a Conservative politician, he has a vested interest in promoting a particular type of viewpoint and may be biased against certain sectors of society. **A:** Portillo does not explain what form the 'encouragement' might take, nor support the claim with evidence, e.g. of other similar successful claims.

b) The claim (that we should be encouraging people to dispose of chewing gum responsibly rather than taxing it) is not reasonable, since a lot of money has to be spent for such campaigns to be successful, and Portillo does not address the question of how it would be financed. He has rejected one possible method of financing such a campaign – taxation. Chewing gum is more of a problem in some areas than others and it is not clear whether he thinks the campaign should be local or national. Even with major publicity, such campaigns may have a limited impact on people's behaviour.

Answers may argue successfully that his claim is reasonable.

ACTIVITY 39

Answers may include some of the following points.

a) The report acknowledges the Old Fox's advertising claim ('try the best'), but is a one-sided report, very critical of the pub's food, although it does also provide some balance by saying that the pub's evening customers probably like it. It gives evidence to support the criticisms (tough beef). The style is meant to entertain ('aerial shots', 'school lunch'), rather than give a factual report. It is in a local newspaper, by a regular reporter, not a well-respected national and famous food critic or chef. It is fairly credible, overall.

b) You would need to know about the writer's experience as a pub/restaurant critic. Does he do this regularly, or is this a one-off? Are his reports always in this critical style, or does he from time to time give positive reviews?

Other answers may be acceptable for a) and b) if supported by reference to the article.

OCR AS Critical Thinking • Unit 1 Guidance to the Activities

ACTIVITY 40

The case of Sergeant Matthews.

a) **What difficulties are there in assessing what actually occurred?**

These documents can be accepted as reliable evidence because they are all formal police documents – they would have been accepted as evidence in court.

The distance of many years makes it difficult to find out what happened. The ways that the police worked in 1932 are unfamiliar, e.g. phoning in from the police box.

The statements available do not give the full picture – there is no record of statements from other people who were in the house.

b) **Use relevant credibility criteria to assess which person is the most credible: Sergeant Matthews, Bert Kent or Fred Larkin.**

In the examination, marks can be obtained for a reasoned judgement that any of these three people is the most credible, provided that it is supported by relevant credibility criteria and reference to the information in the documents.

Sergeant Matthews:
His police record of over 20 years' service, plus the fact he was a sergeant not just a constable, and the commendations on his record suggest trustworthiness, but these events took place some years previously. However, quick thinking when faced with a suicide, or cruelty to a horse enhance his reputation as a police officer, but do not show he did not accept a drink on New Year's Eve. He had a vested interest in the charge against him not being proved, as it would have damaged his career, which weakens the credibility of his evidence. Sergeant Matthews' version of events was corroborated by PC Younger, but the constable would have had a vested interest in not getting himself or his sergeant into trouble. As he worked with the sergeant he is likely to have been biased in his favour.

An inconsistency in Sergeant Matthews' account is that in one place he refers to Larkin's car 'skidding', at another to him driving fast. Otherwise his evidence is consistent. Fred Larkin's statement that Sergeant Matthews did not speak to him about his driving might not have been truthful because he had a vested interest in avoiding getting into trouble for driving whilst unfit through drink.

Superintendent Hook did not find clear evidence that Matthews and Younger had had a drink and he was charged only with failing to report in that he had entered a private house. However, the Superintendent might have been unwilling to damage a fellow police officer's career (showing bias), by pursuing all the avenues of enquiry.

The accounts of what happened given by Sergeant Matthews, PC Younger and Bert Kent corroborate each other in many details. Mrs Kent and Fred Larkin's statements provide further corroboration although both seem to be conveniently ignorant of part of the evening's events. Mrs Kent and Fred Larkin did not directly deny that Sergeant Matthews had had a drink.

c) **Did Sergeant Matthews and PC Younger have a drink at Rockside Boarding House? Did the Sergeant sing a song? What do you think was the most likely course of events?**

Alderman Taylor stated that he had been told that Sergeant Matthews had a drink and sang a song. This sounds most likely – Fred Larkin's statement confirms they knew one another. However, Alderman Taylor's evidence is only hearsay and of itself not sufficient to prove what took place.

Unit 1 Guidance to the Activities OCR AS Critical Thinking

There is no information as to whether there was a 'grudge factor' in Alderman Taylor choosing to repeat to a senior policeman what he had been told. However, an alderman would have been important and respected in the local community.

The events took place in the early hours of 1 January when many people celebrate with a few drinks. The interviews with Bert Kent and Mrs Kent ('It was free house. The sideboard was full of drink') confirm this. Recollections might have been confused by the drink. It is most likely Bert Kent and Sergeant Matthews probably decided together what story to tell.

ACTIVITY 41

1   a) *The Daily Mail* is a major national newspaper and therefore needs to maintain a reputation for fairly accurate reporting of issues. However, it has a vested interest in keeping its readership, so is likely to present issues in a way that will fit in with readers' political opinions and concerns. It is seen as having a right-wing bias and is therefore likely to attack policies originating with the Labour government, or which suggest government interference.

    b) The language of the article is quite emotive – 'the Great Bin Revolt' and 'notorious cowboy car-clamping gangs'. It gives information from two organisations with different perspectives – Defra and the National Family Campaign – but focuses on arguing against the information provided by Defra, rather than giving a neutral report. The use of sources is selective: there is nothing to balance the opinion given by the National Family Campaign.

2   Consider the image in the document. How far is this relevant to the article?

3   Defra is a government department with expertise in matters affecting the environment. However, government departments have to put the government's policies into effect, so cannot be neutral when explaining them.

4   a) Hugh McKinney and the National Family Campaign do not appear to have any expertise in the field of rubbish collection, but do have a vested interest in promoting the interests of their members, families with children, who may have a lot of rubbish and be inconvenienced by the government's proposals. His credibility is therefore weakened.

    b) We would need to know whether he took advice from other members of the National Family Campaign or from someone with expertise in environmental health/bin collections.

    c) The claim is partly reasonable. There are Defra guidelines to follow. Councils generally do not behave like 'cowboy' car clampers and people have routes to complain where council employees behave badly. However, guidelines are not as strong as law or regulation, so the claim is partly reasonable.

    d) Defra's guidelines say bin police should be trained and be subject to criminal record checks. There are also guidelines on the issue of fixed penalty notices.

Unit 1 Section A: Sample answers

Let the punishment fit the crime – baby yobs require baby ASBOs

1.
C Baby yobs should be dealt with by means of baby ASBOs.

2a)
Ev1 Police statistics for 2006 record that 3000 crimes in England and Wales were committed by children under ten.

Ev2 66 of the recorded offences were sex offences.

2b) Other suggested interpretations could include:
- in relation to the total number (millions) of children in England and Wales, the number of crimes is very small.
- 3000 crimes in one year equates to fewer than 10 per day across England and Wales committed by children under ten – which does not indicate child crime is out of control.

2c) These could be strong pieces of evidence because they are taken from police statistics which should be reliable and relevant.

2d) They could be weak pieces of evidence because:
- the majority of reported offences might be minor, e.g. one-off instances of low-level vandalism;
- they relate to *reported* crime committed by children under ten, but not *actual* child criminals – which could be very few.

3.
Paragraph 2: counter-argument

4a) Assumption:
That the fear experienced by women and the elderly is justified by the likelihood of abuse or attack.

4b) The reason in paragraph 3 given to support the main conclusion:
Noisy gangs of tiny thugs make life within their own homes miserable for the people who live in many areas of our towns and cities.

(Other wordings which also say this precisely would be correct.)

5.   Examples.

6.   Reasons:

ASBOs have proved to be a useful tool for hard-pressed police struggling to tackle yobbish behaviour.

The police are completely powerless to take action against those below the age of criminal responsibility.

7a) Counter-assertion.

7b) If children behave as criminal thugs, then they should be dealt with as such.

8.   Reasons that would support an argument against baby ASBOs could include:

ASBOs have been ineffective in reducing crime committed by older children, so would be unlikely to work with younger children.

ASBOs are expensive to operate, so would not be good use of public money.

Most crime committed by young children is not serious and they will grow out of anti-social behaviour in time.

(Other reasons would be accepted, but marks cannot be awarded for simply repeating material in the passage, although it can be drawn on for ideas.)

9. An answer which argued against the reasoning in paragraph 5 supporting the writer's *overall* argument could include the following:

   In the passage the writer argues that child crime is out of control, that police have found ASBOs a useful tool in dealing with yobbish behaviour, and that the police are powerless to deal with criminals aged less than ten. The writer goes on to argue in paragraph 5 that young children who commit crimes should be dealt with as criminals, but does not deal with the key issue, which is whether or not 'baby ASBOs' would work – whether they really would help reduce crime committed by young children. ASBOs are intended to deal with anti-social ('yobbish') behaviour, which is not necessarily the same as criminal acts. The reasoning in paragraph 5 does not support the overall argument.

Unit 1 Section B: Sample answers

Forget moderate exercise, say the health police; get sweaty

1. Only two points would be needed for full marks to be awarded, but answers could include the following or similar material.

   The document draws on claims and evidence from a variety of sources and experts, most of which can be expected to be accurate/reliable, i.e. government/Crown copyright statistical information. *Circulation* (American Hearth Association journal), American College of Sports Medicine, UK Department of Health, Sport England, UK Minister for Sport. Evidence from alternative sources is also used. The Ramblers' Association is a reputable organisation (but represents walkers not health professions); Janet Street-Porter is a *Daily Mail* columnist, rather than a health expert. However, the document includes a range of viewpoints and evidence from the different sources, and the writer deals with them in a way that is balanced. The style of language, apart from the quotation from Janet Street-Porter is not emotive. Overall, the document is credible.

2. The map is not relevant because the issues in the passage are about the effectiveness of different forms of exercise in promoting health. It shows that UK rates of participation in sport for different age groups and areas. It also gives information on the most popular activities. This would be evidence that many people do not take the recommended levels of exercise, but it does not clarify the key issues discussed in the passage.

3. Only two points are needed for full marks to be awarded, but answers must relate to credibility criteria and could include the following, or other, comments:

   David Haslam, as chair of the National Obesity Forum (an independent charity working to improve the prevention and management of obesity), has a vested interest in promoting that organisation, and therefore in ensuring he presents the Forum's viewpoint. (He might lose his role if he failed to promote the Forum's viewpoint.) This weakens his credibility.

   As a representative of a special interest group working in the field of obesity, he is likely to have relevant expertise in the field of exercise and obesity to comment. This strengthens his credibility.

   As chair of an organisation working in the field of obesity, his credibility would already be enhanced by his own reptuation and by that of the organisation. This gives him a motive to make accurate comments. Otherwise his reputation and the National Obesity Forum's would be adversely affected.

4. Answers could include some of the following points:

    We would need to know:
    - if his opinion was representative of other people working in the field of obesity, or whether it was one of a range of opinions;
    - the level/extent of his specialist expertise (and/or access to research in this area) to be able to advise on this issue;
    - how his organisation is funded in order to judge whether or not his opinion is neutral or tainted by vested interest/bias.

5. Answers could include some of the following points:

    Janet Street-Porter is a journalist writing an opinion column rather than a factual article so she has a motive to produce material which will appeal to the readers of the Daily Mail, a popular right-wing newspaper. This weakens her credibility.

    She is a prominent member of the Ramblers' Association so is likely to be biased towards the activity (country walking) that the Association exists to support. This weakens her credibility.

    As a member of the Ramblers' Association she may have (access to) relevant information and expertise about the health benefits of country walking. This would strengthen her credibility.

    As a journalist she would wish to maintain a reputation for independence/neutrality. This could strengthen her credibility.

6a) Marks are awarded for precisely identifying the evidence to support Janet Street-Porter's claim: The UK Department of Health currently recommends 30 minutes of moderate physical exercise at least five times a week, which could include walking.

6b) Answers could argue for or against the claim being reasonable, or something in between, but must be supported by material from the passage. For example:

    Janet Street-Porter's claim (that the best way to avoid heart disease is walking in the countryside) is not reasonable. It is based on a comparison with one activity – running/jogging – not a range of alternative activities. Apart from the claims about wrecking knees and lungs, her reasons for rejecting jogging are not relevant to health and fitness, i.e. running is undignified, she does not want a chest like Paula Radcliffe's, and running is just a way of avoiding human contact. These reasons may be relevant to a personal preference for country walks over other fitness activities, but they do provide strong support for her claim that walking in the countryside is the best way to avoid heart disease.

7. Marks could be awarded for answers which argue that either Janet Street-Porter or the journal *Circulation* is more credible. Answers would not be expected to be as long as that below, which is given to illustrate the range of points responses could cover. Other responses could also be acceptable. To be awarded marks, answers must be supported by material from the passage.

    The journal *Circulation* advocates vigorous activity such as jogging and twice weekly weight training.

    Janet Street-Porter's opinion is closer to the UK government's *current* advice, which recommends five sessions of moderate activity weekly. However the article says the UK government's advice is likely to be brought into line with the American Heart Association. This would provide corroboration of the guidance in *Circulation*.

    The UK government's *current* guidelines are closer to the advice of the National Obesity Forum and it looks likely to adopt the guidelines of the American Heart Association. It this happens in the future, it would provide corroboration of *Circulation*'s position.

According to the passage, writers in the journal are scientists and world leaders in public health and exercise advice. Their relevant expertise, in relation to heart disease, is therefore greater than that of Janet Street-Porter whose expertise relates to country walking. She sees wider benefits from country walks ('spiritual regeneration') as well as avoidance of heart disease.

The journal *Circulation* (and its writers) has a reputation for providing accurate, science-based information. This gives a motive for continuing to provide accurate information, in order to maintain their professional reputation. In this instance, their credibility is greater than that of Janet Street-Porter, even though her reputation is that of an independent journalist.

The National Obesity Forum takes a position that appears similar to Janet Street-Porter in that it says 'gyms aren't a sustainable habit'. However, is not arguing that the guidelines in *Circulation* are wrong – just that they are *unrealistic* for most people. It advocates 'healthy habits'. The National Obesity Forum is perhaps giving advice in the context of wider health issues, not just heart disease, and this is probably the most practical advice for the majority of people.

The journal *Circulation* has greater credibility than Janet Street-Porter as regards advice on avoiding heart disease.

Unit 2 Assessing and Developing Arguments
Section 3 Analysis of Argument

Chapter 7	**Identifying argument components**	**79**
	Worksheet 7.1 Multiple Choice	84
	Worksheet 7.2 Activity	85
	Worksheet 7.3 Activity	86
Chapter 8	**Applying and extending analytical skills**	**87**
	Worksheet 8.1 Key terms: Core	90
	Worksheet 8.2 Activity: Role play	94
	Worksheet 8.3 Core	95

7 Identifying argument components

CHAPTER OVERVIEW

This chapter revises and extends the analytic skills from Unit 1. Students will analyse short passages containing familiar argument components, and learn how to identify intermediate conclusions as part of this analysis. Students will be introduced to common notation to help them with their analysis of argument. Students will also learn to draw conclusions from evidence and short pieces of reasoning.

Analysing more complex arguments

This chapter revises and extends the skills of identifying arguments and analysing arguments into their component parts. The most significant new idea in this chapter is the introduction of intermediate conclusions, which allow candidates to work with considerably more complex arguments. This means that candidates can begin to work with more real-life arguments.

Analysis of short arguments

Student Book Chapter 7 pages 110–129
Specification 3.1.2

Learning objectives

- Distinguish between arguments and other types of writing, e.g. explanations and descriptions (accounts).
- Identify main conclusions and intermediate conclusions and understand the difference between them.
- Identify other argument components in shorter passages including reasons, counter-arguments, evidence and examples.
- Draw conclusions from evidence and short pieces of reasoning.

Common problems

Candidates think they have 'done' analysing arguments and don't need to repeat it.

Candidates struggle with the concept of intermediate conclusion.

Candidates become confused between identifying a conclusion from the passage and drawing a further conclusion (which is not in the passage).

Strategies

Emphasise the increased complexity of argument to be analysed.

Model clearly with your own language the differences between identifying a conclusion which is in the argument and drawing a further conclusion which is not in the argument because it is the next logical step.

Repetition through fun activities such as kinaesthetic, structural activities, such as the activities suggested on the next page, using worksheets 7.2 and 7.3, to make the structure of argument clear.

Suggested activities

Whole class work

Display a claim such as, 'there are many benefits to children from keeping active'. Ask students to suggest reasons that would support this claim, reminding them of the strong logical link required. Give points to students or groups who suggest good reasons, and write them up, labelling them as R1, R2, etc. You should end up with an argument something like this:

R1: Keeping active as a child creates healthy habits to last a lifetime.

R2: Active children learn better than their inactive peers.

R3: Running around/kicking a ball/surfing is fun.

R4: Regular exercise helps to regulate mood, keeping children happy.

C: So there are many benefits to children from keeping active.

Now ask students if there is a further conclusion that could be supported by this reasoning. Someone should suggest something like: 'So children should be encouraged to exercise regularly'.

Show how the first conclusion has become an intermediate conclusion. It is supported by reasons and gives support to a further claim. It is a conclusion drawn on the way to the main conclusion.

This method of thinking through an argument with an eye on structure is also useful as a preparation for students writing their own arguments.

Group activity
Give students a claim and ask them to work through the same process in groups. Claims might include: 'There are many disadvantages to the youth binge drinking culture'; 'There are many advantages to a religious upbringing'; 'Compulsory education has its limits'; 'Advertising is more influential than we like to think'. Use students' own arguments for more analysis practice.

Teacher-led activity
Turn a student's argument into a multiple-choice question. Use the question stem: 'Which of the following is the main conclusion of the argument?' Elicit from students what the main conclusion is and copy it into one of the spaces, A–D. Remind students that the distractors (wrong answers) should be distracting, but must not be right. Ask them what they think would make a good wrong answer. They should suggest intermediate conclusion (this is the most commonly chosen distractor in this sort of question), reasons, conclusions that can be drawn and perhaps assumptions. Cut and paste two reasons and the intermediate conclusion into two more of the answer spaces A–D. Repeat this exercise using question stems such as: 'Which of the following is an intermediate conclusion in the argument?' or 'Which of the following is a counter-assertion in the argument?'

Group activity
Ask groups or pairs of students to write short arguments of 80–100 words using the pattern of reasons, intermediate conclusion and main conclusion. Check the structure. (Alternatively, give them the letters page of a newspaper and ask them to choose a suitable argument.) Ask them to write a multiple-choice question (using one of the question stems you have dealt with). Tell them they must also produce a justification of why the right answer is right and why the wrong answers are wrong. Ask students to answer the finished questions.

Kinaesthetic group activity
Enlarge and photocopy the arguments on Worksheet 7.2. Laminate if you wish to reuse. Guillotine them into component parts. (It works best as an intellectual exercise if you make sure that students cannot do this exercise as a paper jigsaw by matching edges!) Distribute these strips and ask students to find the people who have other components from the same argument. Students must now reconstruct the argument, indicate which element is a reason, intermediate conclusion, etc. and add argument indicators such as *because*, *therefore* and *moreover* to make it coherent. To make this exercise less challenging, you could include component labels (R1, IC, etc.) on the strips with the components.

In their groups students should research evidence and examples on reliable websites and in the library to provide support to the claims in one of the outline arguments. Although students are not required to learn specific evidence for the Unit 2 exam, the more real evidence they have worked with, the better they will understand its role in argument.

Kinaesthetic group activity
Use Worksheet 7.3 for the following Running Dictation activity on drawing conclusions, which practises the skill of deciding which conclusion logically follows from a piece of reasoning. Running dictation trains students' memories, which is useful in the Unit 2 exam when they have to read, remember and manipulate fairly long and complex texts. It also trains them in precision, which is an important Critical

7 Identifying argument components

Thinking skill. It uses aural, oral, written and kinaesthetic learning mechanisms and can easily be differentiated. It can also easily be adapted to multiple-choice questions and can be re-used at intervals throughout the course.

Enlarge and photocopy the texts and conclusions. Guillotine the paper into strips, such that each text is on one strip, and each possible conclusion is on its own strip of paper. Pin the texts around the room. There should be one text for each pair or small group of students. The text should be as far from the students as possible. Mix up the conclusions and lay them out. Tell student A to run (walk carefully avoiding all health and safety risks) to the text, read and memorise as much text as possible, walk back to student B and dictate from memory. Student B must write what A dictates. Then student B should walk to the text, read, memorise, return and dictate to student A. This should continue until students have a word-for-word replica of the text. Shouting, moving the text, taking the paper to the text, etc., are cheating.

Once students have a word-perfect text, they should select and collect the three strips of paper which might be conclusions that could be drawn from their text. They should then decide which one can best be drawn as a conclusion (and write down why), and why the other two cannot. Give all students a printout of all texts and work through the answers with the whole class. Concentrate on students' explanations of why they have made their decisions to help them develop their thinking skills. Even when students give the right answer, it is worth asking, 'Why?'

Guidance to worksheet activities
Multiple choice 7.1

1. d).
2. b) (see analysis below).
3. c) (see analysis below).

CA:(C) [Although] we should oppose the exploitation of children in sweat shops because (R) the minimal pay deprives adults of jobs and the working conditions put children's lives and education at risk.

R: To start with, children in the 10–15 age group need to feel that they are contributing financially to the family, or at least to their own costs.

R: Furthermore, being able to earn money allows them to learn the value of money.

R: We should also not ignore the massive gains in maturity and self-esteem that can come from having an acknowledged and successful role in the adult world, alongside the pains and pleasures of childhood and education.

IC: There are many benefits to young people from working.

C: We should therefore not oppose child labour as such.

Activity 7.2

1. a) IC: It is really important that young people are scientifically literate/C: We should put considerable effort into ensuring that significantly more young people study the sciences for longer.

   b) IC: There are many benefits to GM crops/C: We should research them properly rather than rejecting them through ignorance.

   c) IC: Education is about so much more than exam results/C: We should stop focussing so strongly on students' grades.

   d) IC: Success in life means a great many different things/C: Defining success only in terms of money has negative consequences for society.

   e) IC: There are many benefits to drinking tea/C: It would be good if people drank tea every day.

2. These have been developed into a coherent argument here as an example of how this activity may be done. These answers are a guide only and should not be taken as the only possible way of developing these ideas into an argument.

   a) **Although** many trendy young people see science as uncool, even textile design in the fashion world requires a thorough understanding of the chemistry of fabrics.

For example, one fashion company was recruiting a Product Manager with a degree in Textile Science to ensure that all fabrics used met legal requirements.

Furthermore, the economy depends on a large, skilled workforce, such as young people with the scientific skills to perform medical testing or to develop new energy sources.

In addition to this, future technological progress relies on young people who understand the underlying principles of chemistry, physics and biology. The manufacture of new mobile phones or new hospital equipment, for example, depends on young, creative people with scientific understanding. It is therefore really important that young people are scientifically literate. We should consequently put considerable effort into ensuring that significantly more young people study the sciences for longer.

b) Although many people are suspicious of GM crops, there are many benefits to GM crops. First of all, GM crops can be grown with fewer pesticides. For example, Bt cotton has been modified with poison producing genes which kill the pests that would feed on it, so it does not need to be sprayed. Secondly, GM crops can offer increased yield from the same area of land. Bt Maize, for example, protects the crop against attack by the European Corn Borer (ECB), which can lead to yield losses of 15% or more. Thirdly, GM crops are resistant to many common diseases. Monsanto has developed a virus resistant potato variety, for example. We should, therefore, research GM crops properly rather than rejecting them through ignorance.

c) We should stop focussing so strongly on students' grades because education is about so much more than exam results. One reason for this is that education can – and should – expand young people's minds. For example, it should encourage people to think about what is the right thing to do, not just what is the right answer. Furthermore, education can give young people new horizons. Moreover, education can help each young person find the right path in life for them, whether that path is, for instance, music or medicine. Additionally, education can be a way forward for people in troubled times such as illness or bereavement. Finally, continuing to learn can help older people remain healthy, active and alert for longer.

d) Many people see success in life as making lots of money. However, working with drug addicts to help turn their lives around might represent success for one person. Remaining married to someone you love through a difficult period might represent success for other people. Some people see success as growing the biggest marrow in the village. So we can see that success in life means a great many different things. Furthermore, if we define success only in terms of money, people's other successes will feel less satisfying. Added to this, people need recognition for their own successes. Therefore defining success only in terms of money has negative consequences for society.

e) Tea has anti-biotic properties which help prevent infection. In addition, tea contains anti-oxidants which are thought to help prevent cancer. There are, therefore, many benefits to drinking tea. Therefore it would be good if people drank tea every day.

Activity 7.3

a) iii) can be concluded. It is a very weak conclusion.
   i) is too strong to be supported by the limited evidence. In particular there is no evidence to suggest that this will happen soon.
   ii) is far too strong. At most the evidence could be used to support the claim that rats could join sniffer dogs in rescue teams. (You may wish to ask candidates to give reasons why rats might not replace dogs).

b) i) can be concluded. The evidence relates specifically to burger chains, and relates to cost cutting. Because burger chains are interested in cutting costs and maximising profit, we can conclude that they are likely to invest in this technology.

ii) cannot be concluded because we do not have reason to believe that all restaurants could benefit. The technology works for fast food outlets because they have a limited menu and a variety of customers, and research indicates that a family car producing two tall and two small people is likely to lead to an order for chicken nuggets, whereas a truck with one large person is likely to lead to an order for a Big Mac.

iii) cannot be concluded because it is not in any way supported by the evidence.

c) iii) can be concluded, because the new rations mean that soldiers would not have to carry the weight of the water around.

i) may be true (at least of inexperienced soldiers) but nothing in the passage gives us reason to believe this.

ii) is true if the swamp water or urine is unfiltered, but the point of the passage is that this new technology allows only water and not bugs to pass the membrane.

d) iii) can be concluded.

i) is absurd.

ii) rephrases a reason in the passage, that these disinfectants would be eco-friendly.

7.1 Multiple Choice

1. **Read the passage below.**
   Fans of Indie bands are increasingly likely to try to sabotage the rise of manufactured *X Factor*-style Christmas no. 1s by purchasing symbolic downloads. The real problem with *X Factor* Christmas singles is that they are not even Christmassy. The last great Christmas single was Mariah Carey's 'All I Want for Christmas is You' in 1994.

   Is it best described as:

   a) an argument.

   b) an explanation.

   c) a quarrel.

   d) unconnected sentences.

   You should refer to the following text for questions 2 and 3.
   Although we should oppose the exploitation of children in sweat shops because the minimal pay deprives adults of jobs and the working conditions put children's lives and education at risk, there are many benefits to young people from working. To start with, children in the 10–15 age group need to feel that they are contributing financially to the family, or at least to their own costs. Furthermore, being able to earn money allows them to learn the value of money. We should also not ignore the massive gains in maturity and self-esteem that can come from having an acknowledged and successful role in the adult world, alongside the pains and pleasures of childhood and education. We should therefore not oppose child labour as such.

2. **Which of the following is an intermediate conclusion?**

   a) Children in the 10–15 age group need to feel that they are contributing financially to the family.

   b) There are many benefits to young people from working.

   c) We should oppose the exploitation of children in sweat shops.

   d) We should therefore not oppose child labour as such.

3. **Which of the following is the conclusion of the counter-argument?**

   a) The minimal pay deprives adults of jobs.

   b) The working conditions put children's lives and education at risk.

   c) We should oppose the exploitation of children in sweat shops.

   d) We should therefore not oppose child labour as such.

7 Identifying argument components

7.2 Activity

1. Identify the intermediate and main conclusions in outline arguments a)–e).

2. Write these outline arguments as coherent arguments including argument indicators. In at least one argument add evidence you have researched on the Internet or in the library.

   a) Even textile design in the fashion world requires a thorough understanding of the chemistry of fabrics.
   We should put considerable effort into ensuring that significantly more young people study the sciences for longer.
   It is really important that young people are scientifically literate.
   The economy depends on a large, skilled workforce.
   Future technological progress relies on young people who understand the underlying principles of chemistry, physics and biology.

   b) GM crops can offer increased yield from the same area of land.
   We should research them properly rather than rejecting them through ignorance.
   GM crops are resistant to many common diseases.
   There are many benefits to GM crops.
   GM crops can be grown with fewer pesticides.

   c) Education is about so much more than exam results.
   Education can – and should – expand young people's minds.
   Education can give young people new horizons.
   Education can help each young person find the right path in life for them.
   We should stop focussing so strongly on students' grades.
   Education can be a way forward for people in troubled times such as illness or bereavement.
   Continuing to learn can help older people remain healthy, active and alert for longer.

   d) Success in life means a great many different things.
   People need recognition for their own successes.
   Defining success only in terms of money has negative consequences for society.
   Working with drug addicts to help turn their lives around might represent success for one person.
   Remaining married to someone you love through a difficult period might represent success for other people.
   Some people see success as growing the biggest marrow in the village.
   If we define success only in terms of money, people's other successes will feel less satisfying.

   e) It would be good if people drank tea every day.
   Tea has antibiotic properties which help prevent infection.
   Tea contains antioxidants which are thought to help prevent cancer.
   There are many benefits to drinking tea.

7.3 Activity

1. **Decide which conclusion can best be drawn from each passage. Justify your decision.**

   a) Rats have an extremely sensitive sense of smell, and can crawl just about anywhere. They can be taught to home in on people, and it is possible to fit them with radios which transmit their brainwaves.

   i) Rats could soon be helping to locate earthquake survivors buried in the wreckage of collapsed buildings.

   ii) Rats are likely to replace sniffer dogs in rescue teams.

   iii) A rat trained to recognise the smell of humans can reach areas that dogs cannot get to.

   b) A computer called Bob can predict your McDonald's order by looking at your car and your height. Chefs are able to start cooking food before you order it based on these predictions. Burgers are served hotter, waiting times have been cut by about 1 minute and waste has been virtually eliminated.

   i) Burger chains are likely to invest in this predictive technology.

   ii) All restaurants should invest in this predictive technology.

   iii) It is immoral to invest in technology to cut waiting times at McDonald's when there are starving people in the world.

   c) Food scientists working for the US military have developed a dried food ration which troops can hydrate by adding the filthiest of muddy swamp water or even urinating on it. A semi-permeable membrane allows only water molecules to pass through. The new rations weigh 0.4kg for a day's food, whereas hydrated rations weigh 3.5kg.

   i) Most soldiers would rather carry more weight than urinate on their food.

   ii) Soldiers may become very ill if they use swamp water or urine.

   iii) Soldiers would benefit from much lighter burdens with the new rations.

   d) Surplus or waste wine and poor quality wine made from sour grapes can be turned into efficient and eco-friendly disinfectants. Added to salt and sulphur dioxide the wine mixture is much better at killing food-borne bacteria on kitchen surfaces than conventional disinfectants.

   i) We should drink wine to kill bacteria inside us.

   ii) It would be environmentally friendly to use sour wine disinfectants.

   iii) We should consider using such alternative disinfectants.

8 Applying and extending analytical skills

CHAPTER OVERVIEW

This chapter extends students' analytical skills further. Students will analyse longer passages containing familiar and new argument components, including principles and analogies. Students will revise and extend their understanding of inconsistency and extend their specialist vocabulary.

Greater complexity and authenticity

This chapter extends students' analytical skills to cover longer passages with more complex components. The passages in the Unit 2 exam are more complex than those in the Unit 1 exam. Although the exam passages are manipulated, students' skills should enable them to approach some authentic material by this stage. They can certainly develop their skills by working with real arguments from quality newspapers and magazines.

Analysis of short arguments

Student Book Chapter 8 pages 130–145
Specification 3.2.1

Learning objectives
- Identify analogies.
- Identify principles.
- Identify a range of elements in longer texts.
- Identify inconsistency and contradiction.
- Use technical and semi-technical terms accurately.

Common problems
Students find analysis rather dry.

Students struggle to identify principles and analogies in exam conditions.

Students are inclined to forget their structural understanding and focus on gist.

Students' language skills let them down; they tend, for example, to be vague, and to approximate to a gist understanding, rather than using language precisely.

Some of them may need to strengthen their reading and writing skills.

Strategies
Mix analysis with animated discussions and development of argument.

Organise lessons around interesting topics, but repeatedly refocus on analytical skills.

Use students' own work for analysis practice.

Repeatedly revise the key terms and definitions so that students understand the questions in the exam.

Teach language and vocabulary skills.

Suggested activities

Key terms
Start lessons with a short activity involving key terms – games can be an entertaining and educational start to a lesson. Using Worksheet 8.1, play 'key terms bingo' in which students write down three, six or nine key terms in a bingo grid and you read out the definitions. Play a definitions games in which students choose a word to explain, and others in the group have to guess what it is. Hold up a bag and explain that three key terms have become lost in there and need to be rescued. Ask students to guess which. They could give you either words or definitions. Keep enlarged key terms lists on the wall and allow students to refer to them, praising good use of available resources.

Give students versions of Worksheet 8.1 from the CD-ROM with missing words or definitions and ask them to fill in the blanks. This worksheet contains a selection of key terms which are most likely to appear in exam questions. You may wish to add to it.

Optional word and logic filler
Write the following symbols on the board:

? = correct

X = incorrect

? = correct letter is later in the alphabet

* = correct letter is earlier in the alphabet.

Tell students that you have a four-letter word in mind and they have to guess it. Elicit any polite four-letter word from students and write it on the board. Underneath, write a symbol for each letter. So, if your word was 'work' and a student had suggested 'play' you would write, '? ? ? *' to indicate that the first three letters should be later in the alphabet than 'p', 'l' and 'a', and the fourth letter should be earlier in the alphabet than 'y'. Students think, then suggest another word that fits these criteria. You respond with symbols and the game proceeds until students work out the right word. Although this activity does not focus on a specific exam still it helps students to focus on words and logical processes of thought. Once they understand it, they can play in small groups between activities or at the beginning or end of a lesson.

Role play
Working through activities based on Worksheet 8.2 should help students to use their analytical and logical skills in a creative situation. This should help them to internalise these skills.

The situation: the local council in Helton – a small town away from major centres, which has a 1960's concrete precinct – has a small budget for improving the town centre and facilities available to local people. It has asked a number of people what they dislike or find problematic about Helton.

Put students into small groups and give each group the information about one person from Helton.

Task 1: Based on the resident's complaints, write a list of positive recommendations that your character would see as improvements to Helton town centre.

Task 2: Write an argument to support the conclusion that these recommendations should be adopted and put into action by the council.

Task 3: Groups should analyse each others' arguments into evidence, reasons, intermediate and main conclusions.

Task 4: Stage a meeting between the council and the residents. One student from each group should represent their character and put their views forward. Encourage the most able students to argue freely based on previous work rather than just reading their written arguments. They should attempt to counter others' arguments.

Task 5: Mix the groups by taking one person from each existing group to form a new group. The new group is now the council executive, and their task is to come up with a plan of action to improve Helton town centre. They should consider principles that might help them to decide between competing claims for the money (e.g. We need to be fair to all parties/The needs of the young are most important). They should make specific recommendations and write an argument to support these recommendations. If there is time, and students have artistic flair, they could produce drawings to accompany their proposal.

Task 6: Students should analyse their arguments. They should turn the project into a display with reasons backed on blue, conclusion on red, intermediate conclusions on green and other elements on yellow.

Guidance to worksheet activities
8.3 Core

1. So we should change the system to promote feelings of success.

2. Exams are not actually as important as the system makes us believe.

3. We should act in everybody's best interests.

4. The situation of it being silly to let it worry you for 30 years that you can't run as fast as an Olympic sprinter is compared with the situation of it being silly to work yourself into a state because you haven't got ten A*s at GCSE.

8 Applying and extending analytical skills

5. It is inconsistent to say that getting good exam grades has helped us to get good jobs and also to say that exams do not actually have much effect on our adult lives.

6. Encourage students to start working towards the type of argument they will need to write under timed conditions as practise helps. Suggest that they limit themselves to 100–150 words and concentrate on structure and precision. The following argument is provided as an example of the kind of argument that students should be aiming at, at this stage of the course.

Although exam results are important because they might help you to get an interesting or well-paid job, mental health, physical health and happiness all count for far more than exam results. Poor mental health can lead to far more problems than poor exam results. Depression, anxiety and stress, for example, significantly reduce both quality of life and life expectancy. Furthermore, if your physical health does not allow you to work or to enjoy your free time, your quality of life will suffer more than if you failed an exam. It is, moreover, possible to be poor and under-qualified but happy, or to be well-qualified and well off, but unhappy. Evidence suggests that highly qualified people are giving up high-powered jobs to seek simpler, happier lives.

8.1 Key terms: Core

Argument	Attempt to persuade a reader (or listener) to accept something. An argument must have a conclusion and at least one reason.
Analyse argument	Breaking an argument down into its component parts and label them.
Evaluate argument	Say how well the reasoning works by considering appeals, flaws, the use of evidence, examples and explanations, and patterns of reasoning such as analogy, hypothetical reasoning and the use of principles.
Principle	A general, rule-like statement that applies beyond the immediate circumstances and acts as a guide to action.
Analogy	A form of argument that uses parallels between similar situations to persuade the audience to accept a conclusion.
Refute	Show that arguments do not work – highlight the weakness; perhaps by showing them to be inconsistent.
Repudiate	Condemn an opinion, reject as unfounded or inapplicable.
Strong conclusion	A conclusion that is very specific and tightly defined. Claims a great deal and requires a lot of support. May include words such as 'all' 'always' 'never'.
Strong argument	Has reasons that give us grounds for accepting the conclusion and strong logical links. No flaw.

(Continued overleaf)

8.1 Key terms: Core

(cont.)

Weak conclusion	A conclusion that is not very specific or tightly defined.
Weak argument	Has reasons that do not give us grounds for accepting the conclusion or uses irrelevant or unreliable evidence. There may be inconsistency, flaws or irrelevance, and the logical links of support do not hold together.
Knowledge	True belief, and can be objectively verified.
Belief	Something that is held to be true but may not be objectively verified.
Necessary condition	Condition that must happen for something to be the case.
Sufficient condition	Condition that is enough to ensure that something will be the case.
Inference	Logical link between reasons and conclusion such that the conclusion follows, or can be drawn from, the reasons.
Challenge	If you challenge a conclusion you argue against it.
Inconsistent	When evidence or an argument contains two claims which cannot both be correct at the same time.

(Continued overleaf)

8.1 Key terms: Core

(*cont.*)

Ambiguous	Can have more than one meaning and it is not clear which meaning is intended in a particular context.
Converse	The opposite of something which is expressed or implied..
Imply	To lead to something as a logical consequence.
Coherent	An argument in which all the logical links are strong would be described as '……'
Structure	The way an argument is put together into a logical shape.
Opinion	Something someone believes.
Challenge	To oppose a claim or argument.
Counter	To oppose a claim or argument and show why it is wrong.
Assess	Like evaluate, this means to weigh up, to decide how well something (an argument) works.

(*Continued overleaf*)

8.1 Key terms: Core

(cont.)

Reasoning	Structured, logical thought, often in the form of an argument.
Contradict	A special form of inconsistency. Ideas or facts which say exactly the opposite things.
Draw a conclusion	Consider the next logical step – decide what (further) conclusion can be supported by some reasons, some evidence or an argument.

8.2 Activity: Role play

Emma, 15

It's a bit boring for me really. There is a youth club but it meets in a dingy room at the top of two flights of stairs. Even the library is on the first floor over the shops. And there's no lift. I can only go if there are people to carry me and my wheelchair. Sometimes that makes me cringe, so I just stay at home. I can't get to the shops either because of those steps. And I find all the hoodies and drunks hanging round quite threatening.

Mike, 17

They're always moaning at us for skating and hanging round in the precinct, but there's nowhere else. There's no skate park or nothing. The youth club's for little kids who want to play games and do pop karaoke – you know, playing at being grown up. Me and my mates, we need somewhere to hang out, listen to proper music and play pool and that. This place is dead. There's no life, no soul, just concrete. And they fine us for our wall art. Call it vandalism.

Karen, 27

This is such a rubbish place if you're stuck at home with young kids. You can't take a buggy out, there's steps everywhere. And there's no facilities. No park for miles, no play groups, no ball pits. The only leisure centre's six miles away, and the buses practically don't exist, and anyway there's no crèche, and the children's pool is tiny. I do drive over there, but Chris needs the car most days, so I'm stuck. And the concrete. There isn't a single tree. It's not surprising the gangs are starting to cause trouble.

Jasvinder, 22

I do voluntary youth work with some of the kids from the housing estate and the whole system is just failing them from the moment they're born. Look at it, it's a concrete prison. There's nothing here. No support system. There's no funding for projects working with art or music or drama or gardening to give people's lives some meaning. Everyone is stuck in their own little bubble, not really playing their part in a community. I'm sure if we got things right for the kids we wouldn't have such a problem with homelessness.

Edie, 87

They don't provide for pensioners like me. Look at those steps up to the precinct, they're like a mountain. I do envy those young men leaping around. They intimidate me, I'm never quite sure whether they're going to have my purse, but there's a couple of them will help with my shopping and they're quite polite really. Just bored, I expect, and I can see why. There's no community any more. Even the café closed so you can't get a sausage butty and a cup of tea. I'd like to meet more people – but not just people like me who are nearly dead, young people who'd make me feel alive – and be part of something, but there just isn't anywhere I can walk to and there are no buses to speak of. It's a very lonely place to get old.

Phoebe, 17

This place is a cultural desert. No art, no music, no theatre. Nowhere for people like me to meet and talk about things. I don't want to be forced into the drugs and drink scene but sometimes I'm so bored I think it might be the only way to escape. You can't even go shopping here. You have to get the bus 16 miles to Porton. But then there might not be a bus back till next week.

8.3 Core

Read the passage and answer the questions below.

The exam system tends to make most of us – even the most apparently successful – feel a failure. A study of 5000 15-year-old children showed that 38% of high-achieving girls and 19% of boys experienced exam-related stress, anxiety and depression. Most of us have, at some point in our lives, dreamed about exam failure and, for many of us, this feeling lingers into adult life, despite having good jobs as a result of getting good grades in exams. 1

Yet exams are not actually as important as the system makes us believe. To start with, they do not actually have that much effect on our adult lives. By the time you are 39 and a successful plumber, designer, secretary or company manager, no one cares about your GCSE grades. Actually, even by the time you get to your first job after university, no one cares about your GCSE grades. So what if you only got a D in a really dull subject they forced you to take? 2

Personal qualities such as hard work, determination and imagination are more likely than exam grades to affect your success at work. Amanda, for example, did not perform very well in her GCSEs but got a job with a bank and discovered that she was very good at creative marketing and working with people. She was reliable and persistent, and is now a marketing manager. She is only one of many who do better in the real world than in the artificial world of exams. 3

Exams do not make a real difference to our everyday lives in adulthood. Mental health, physical health and happiness all count for far more than exam results. You don't let it worry you for 30 years that you can't run as fast as an Olympic sprinter. It is equally silly working yourself into a state because you haven't got ten A*s at GCSE. 4

We should act in everybody's best interests. So we should change the system to promote feelings of success. 5

1. Identify the main conclusion of the argument below.

2. Identify the intermediate conclusion in the argument.

3. Identify a principle used in the argument.

4. Identify the situations compared in the analogy in paragraph 4.

5. Identify an inconsistency in the argument.

6. 'Mental health, physical health and happiness all count for far more than exam results.' Write a short argument to support or challenge this claim.

Section 4 Evaluating Argument

Chapter 9	Evaluating reasoning: the use of evidence, examples and explanation	97
	Worksheet 9.1 Foundation Core	100
	Worksheet 9.2 Longer text: Core	101
Chapter 10	Evaluating reasoning: appeals	103
	Worksheet 10.1 Foundation	105
Chapter 11	Evaluating reasoning: flaws	107
	Worksheet 11.1 Core	110
	Worksheet 11.2 Extension	113
Chapter 12	Evaluating reasoning: analogies, hypothetical reasoning and principles	114
	Worksheet 12.1 Extension	117

9 Evaluating reasoning: the use of evidence, examples and explanations

OCR AS Critical Thinking

CHAPTER OVERVIEW

In this chapter students will begin to evaluate arguments. They will learn to evaluate the use of evidence and examples and consider alternative explanations. The focus of this evaluation is on the use of these components to support reasons and conclusions.

Evaluation of evidence, examples and explanations

Evaluation is the skill of judging whether an argument is strong or weak; whether the evidence, examples, explanations and reasons give us sufficient grounds to accept a conclusion. The focus in Unit 2 is on the use of evidence, examples and explanations to support a conclusion. Weak use of evidence would include:

- evidence not being precisely focused on the reason or conclusion it supports
- evidence being insufficient to support a conclusion.

Weak use of examples would include:

- examples that do not precisely illustrate the situation at issue
- examples that are not typical or representative.

Weak use of explanations would include:

- partial or incorrect explanation
- ignoring other plausible explanations.

Analysis of longer arguments

Student Book Chapter 9 pages 146–163
Specification 3.2.2

Learning objectives

- Evaluate the use of evidence in argument.
- Evaluate the use of examples in argument.
- Evaluate the use of explanations in argument.

Common problems

Students are inclined to consider whether the evidence is true rather than whether it supports a reason or conclusion. Students would like to produce standard answers that they can pre-learn, rather than responding to the precise evidence, examples or information they have in front of them.

Strategies

Use careful questioning to ensure that students understand that in Unit 2 they need to evaluate the use of evidence. They need to consider whether the evidence gives us grounds to accept a reason or conclusion *if* the evidence is true.

Students need plenty of practice in articulating their own thoughts about specific pieces of evidence, supported by some general ideas of the sorts of things they should be looking for.

Suggested activities

Teacher-led class activity

Remind students that 'plausible' means 'possible', could happen, not far-fetched. Ask students to write 'Plausible' on one side of a piece of paper, and 'Implausible' on the other. Give students a piece of numerical evidence or information, for example: 'A crop circle has appeared in a field in Wiltshire'. Ask them to write a (plausible) explanation. Get students to read out their explanations and ask the class to vote on whether it seems plausible or implausible by holding up their sheets of paper with the appropriate word showing.

Multiple-choice questions

Refer to the multiple-choice questions on the CD-ROM, or use the questions online at www.cie.org.uk/thinkingskills. Choose several questions with the stem: 'Which of the following, if true, would most strengthen/weaken the argument?'

To make the multiple-choice practice more fun, turn it into a game. Various familiar formats based on well-known quiz shows can work with points or prizes for success. Alternatively, allow candidates to place virtual bets on the outcome. Either of these makes the process interactive and fun and holds students' attention.

Class activity leading to group work

Write the price of two pieces of chicken from a supermarket on the board – one organic, the other intensively farmed. (Late 2007 prices: £17.79 per kg organic; £7.94 per kg intensively farmed.)

Ask whether this difference in price is justified/whether students would be prepared to spend the extra (or eat less meat in order to fund the difference). Ask students to support their positions.

Using a projector, go to www.ethicalmatrix.net. This site includes a free teacher and student guide. It provides a way of making decisions and a great deal of evidence about the conditions of intensively versus organically farmed fish, chicken and pigs. Work through the exercise on chicken, allowing students to read the information and democratically agree answers to the questions. Ask if the exercise has made anyone change their minds. Get them to explain why.

Ask students to work through one of the remaining exercises, on either pigs or fish, in pairs or small groups. In the group, they should write an argument of 80–100 words, with a focus on using evidence to support reasons. They should analyse the argument and edit it to make improvements. Be strict about the word count – it helps students to consider what is absolutely necessary, what is not and how to avoid repetition. Students should then write the question and four possible answers and, on a separate page, a justification of why the right answer is right and the wrong answer is wrong. If students email their questions to you, you can put them together and get students to answer them.

Guidance to worksheet activities

9.1 Foundation: Core

Answers could include the following.

1. a) Men generally don't go to the doctor's until it's too late, whereas women tend go as soon as they notice a problem; men tend to take more risks than women; women are naturally hardier than men; men stop working when they retire and don't fill the gap in their lives with other interests.

b) Work is more interesting than changing nappies; humans are social beings and staying at home with children can be very isolating so work provides a better social situation.

c) There is a common chemical structure to nice smelling or nasty smelling substances; there is a common biological or evolutionary origin to our sense of smell.

d) People need to show off; demonstrate their social status through their gadgets.

e) The journalists were not using their own phones so the messages couldn't be traced back to individuals, whereas employees were using their own phones and messages could be traced back to individuals; journalists are not necessarily interested in the details of communications technology or engineering, whereas employees are likely to have some interest and therefore be more engaged; journalists do not depend on the company for their income, and are therefore more at liberty to be rude than employees, who do depend on the company for their income.

2. a) The passage explains the claim that isolation worsens an area's economic prospects and uses this claim as a reason to support the conclusion that isolated neighbourhoods in big cities should be reconnected. So it is explanation supporting argument.

b) The Venetian Ghetto is currently economically deprived.

c) The example seems to be precisely relevant, about exactly the same thing as the situation at issue. As far as we know, the road widening was the only change, but we would need to investigate whether there were other socio-economic changes which could have led to the increase in deprivation.

9 Evaluating reasoning: the use of evidence, examples and explanations — OCR AS Critical Thinking

9.2 Longer text: Core

Answers could include the following.

1. The author uses a statistic about household reductions in emissions to support a claim about personal emissions so this evidence is not precisely relevant.

2. It is reasonable to use this statistic/example to shock us into realising the effect of our laziness or carelessness in terms of our emissions and effect on the planet.

It is not reasonable to use the example of a citizen of Burundi to compare with a UK citizen because the author is trying to persuade us that we can significantly lower our emissions without significantly altering our lifestyle. But a citizen of Burundi has a significantly lower standard of living than a UK citizen so the comparison does not seem reasonable.

3. The author recommends buying a smaller, more efficient to reduce emissions from driving without giving up cars, yet also recommends delaying buying a new car because of emissions. You can't do both of these, so it's not actually as easy as he claims to reduce emissions from driving.

4. Taking public transport to work is not travelling less, it is travelling differently so, the evidence is not relevant to the claim that we should travel less. The evidence does, however, clearly support the claim that we should travel less by plane.

5. One explanation for this might be cheap, easily obtainable flights.

Another might be that, culturally, the British are more likely to fly abroad, whereas many Americans do not fly at all, significantly reducing their national average.

Credit other plausible explanations.

6. In terms of attitude and scale, taxation does seem to be a reasonable comparison with emissions reduction.

However, taxation is not a choice, whereas the article is portraying emissions reduction as something we should be able to choose.

7. a) Some of the examples and evidence are precisely focussed on the claim that we can significantly reduce our emissions without significantly altering our lifestyle – credit any two well-expressed examples such as the following.

Efficient boiler and wood-burning stove are both good ways of cutting emissions without changing our lifestyle.

Taking short showers and unplugging gadgets are both ways of reducing emissions quite a bit with only minimal lifestyle change.

b) Some of the examples are not so precisely focussed on the claim because they would require a change in lifestyle which could be regarded as significant:

For instance, taking public transport instead of driving is a significant change in lifestyle, and can be quite a lot less comfortable.

Eating locally produced, fresh, organic and vegan food instead of imported, meat and dairy-based processed food would require significantly greater lifestyle changes – more cooking, more effort into shopping, for example.

c) Overall, the author has done enough to show that some minor lifestyle changes can have a significant effect on our emissions, and that some bigger lifestyle changes can also have a significant effect.

8. The author has done quite a lot to persuade us with good reasons that it is worth us reducing our emissions, even though China and India are not:

– partly because this can be done fairly easily,

– partly because the cumulative effect of many people making these changes is huge, and

– partly because countries such as China and India could begin to use low carbon technologies and work towards a long-term, worldwide solution.

However, for the argument to fully support the claim, we would also need to accept that our reduction would create a 'space' for China's and India's emissions – that there is a maximum level of emissions that will not damage the environment.

9.1 Foundation: core

1. Suggest plausible explanations for the following claims and situations.

   a) Men have an average life expectancy about six years shorter than women.

   b) Mothers are happier if they work.

   c) People around the world generally find the same smells pleasant and the same smells unpleasant.

   d) People frequently replace gadgets which work perfectly well.

   e) Nokia recently let journalists at its Research and Development centre at Oulu in Finland borrow the latest multimedia phones during an open day with speeches by leading technology engineers. They were encouraged to send text messages with questions and comments for a real-time display on a giant display behind the speaker during the speeches. The screen soon became a giant message board with rude, amusing and irrelevant comments which distracted from the speeches. Afterwards, a Nokia spokesperson said, 'We used the system for an internal meeting last week, and all the comments were very sensible. We were surprised at how different it was today.'

   New Scientist, November 2007, p. 92

2. Read the passage below, then complete a)–c).

   Sociologists think that isolation worsens an area's economic prospects by reducing opportunities for commerce. Laura Vaughan at University College London analysed street-by-street poverty in London over the past century and showed that inaccessible areas attract poorer inhabitants. Analysis of Venice by Volchenkov and Blanchard has shown that most areas of the city can be accessed by 100 random turns on the canals. It takes around 300 random steps to reach the Venetian Ghetto, created in 1516 to separate Jews from Christians. A further example is pointed out by Geoffrey Ingarfield, a housing expert in the UK. 'The widening of the A13 in Newham, London, completely isolated the area to the immediate south, causing shops and the last secondary school to close. Unable to cross the road, the people to the south became more isolated and socially deprived.' Isolated neighbourhoods in big cities should be reconnected, perhaps by building tunnels and bridges and improving public transport networks.

   New Scientist, 3 November 2007, p. 8

   a) Is the passage above an argument, an explanation, an argument supported by explanation or none of these?

   b) What additional piece of information would you need in order for the evidence about the Venetian Ghetto to support the claim that, 'isolation worsens an area's economic prospects'?

   c) Evaluate the strength of the example of the A13 in Newham.

9.2 Longer text: Core

Read the text below, then complete questions 1–9.

1 Many people ask whether it is worth trying to cut our carbon emissions when countries like China and India are increasing their emissions so rapidly. The answer has to be: 'Yes it is.' Chris Goodall, author of *How to Live a Low Carbon Life*, reckons it is possible to cut individual emissions by around 75% without seriously altering our lifestyles. For a western European, that means slashing personal emissions from about 12 tonnes of carbon dioxide to just 3 tonnes.

2 You can cut heating-related emissions by 40% or more by replacing an inefficient old-style boiler with a condensing model, by improving house insulation and by turning down the thermostat by 2°C in winter. Installing a wood burning stove in the living room provides attractive heat from a renewable source and could cut household emissions by 2 tonnes of CO_2, which is almost a quarter of the total cut necessary.

3 It is also simple to reduce emissions and halve electricity by taking simple measures. Take short showers instead of baths, don't use a tumble dryer, do use energy efficient light bulbs. Switching to a laptop instead of a desktop could save you 0.2 tonnes of carbon dioxide. A digital TV set-top box on standby uses enough energy to emit 0.06 tonnes of CO_2 in a year (roughly the total emissions of an average citizen of Burundi), so you can save most of that by unplugging every time you turn the TV off.

4 It is also easy to reduce our emissions from driving without actually giving up our cars. Buying a smaller, more efficient car running on diesel or LPG could cut emissions by up to 0.4 tonnes per car per year. Turning off car air conditioning can save 0.1 tonnes, while driving moderately and at fuel-efficient speeds will enable some drivers to cut emissions by 0.2 tonnes per year. Another idea is to delay buying a new car. A typical car takes between 3 and 5 tonnes of CO_2 to manufacture. So even if the new model would be more fuel-efficient, it is probably better to put off buying it.

5 The bottom line is that we should all travel less. Taking public transport to work is an excellent way of reducing emissions. With every 1500 km you commute, you save 0.5 tonnes of CO_2. Frequent flyers have carbon footprints ten times bigger than the rest of us. Britons are the worst offenders in the world for this, with average emissions equivalent to 1.6 tonnes of CO_2 per person – double that of the average American.

6 Food makes up a surprising proportion of our carbon footprint. It makes up about 2 tonnes of CO_2 per person. By buying local, organic, vegan food, you could strip about 1.7 tonnes of this. Recycling cans and buying drinks in glass or recyclable plastic containers can help further.

7 By making these small changes, the average western European can cut nearly 8 tonnes from their personal carbon footprint. Multiply that by enough people and the impact could be significant. If just one-third of the UK population did the same, it would save 160 million tonnes of CO_2, or more than a quarter of the nation's emissions. Emissions reductions are a bit like taxes. You may not like them, and your individual contribution may seem too small to matter, but multiply them by several million, and you can start to move mountains.

8 Scaled up to global level, these cuts become highly significant. If 100 million people in richer nations cut their CO_2 emissions by 10 tonnes per year, on average, that would save a billion tonnes of CO_2 emissions a year. This would create space for China and India to grow their economies and their carbon emissions for another year. Then we would need to add another 100 million people for the next year, and so on until new low-carbon technologies become cheap enough for developing countries like China and India to adopt them without undermining their economic development.

New Scientist, November 2007, pp. 34–41

9.2 Longer text: Core

1. Identify one weakness in the use of evidence relating to cutting personal emissions by almost quarter using wood burning stoves.

2. Is it reasonable to use the example of a citizen of Burundi to compare with a UK citizen? Justify your answer.

3. Identify an inconsistency in paragraph 4.

4. Does the evidence in paragraph 5 support the claim that we should all travel less? Why (not)?

5. Britons have the highest emissions in the world from flying. Suggest one explanation for this.

6. Is it reasonable to use the example of taxation to compare with cuts in emissions? Justify your answer.

7. The text claims that it is possible to cut individual emissions significantly without seriously affecting our lifestyle.

    a) Explain two strengths in the use of evidence and examples to support this claim.

    b) Explain two weaknesses in the use of evidence and examples to support this claim.

    c) Overall, do you think that the author has supported this claim?

8. Does the author do enough to support the claim that it is worth trying to cut our carbon emissions even though countries like China and India are rapidly increasing theirs?

9. Do you try to minimise your carbon footprint? Explain why (not). Then write an argument to support your standpoint. Does this make you rethink your position?

10 Evaluating reasoning: appeals

CHAPTER OVERVIEW

In this chapter students will continue to evaluate arguments. They will learn to evaluate the use of appeals to something or someone beyond the argument. They will learn to explain why emotive or irrelevant appeals, or attempts to end an argument with an appeal are weak forms of argument.

Evaluating appeals

Evaluation is the skill of judging whether an argument is strong or weak. In the case of appeals evaluation is the skill of judging whether the appeal is relevant, whether it involves reason or only emotion, and whether it is used to support or to end argument. Candidates need to be able to recognise five different patterns of reasoning:

- appeal to authority
- appeal to popularity
- appeal to tradition
- appeal to history
- appeal to emotion.

At AS Level, students need to be aware that an appeal can be strong, but the focus is on being able to explain why a weak appeal does not provide much support for a conclusion.

Analysis of longer arguments

Student Book Chapter 10 pages 164–175
Specification 3.2.2

Learning objectives

- Understand the meaning of the term 'appeal'. Recognise appeals within arguments.
- Identify and evaluate:
    ? appeal to authority
    ? appeal to popularity
    ? appeal to tradition
    ? appeal to history
    ? appeal to emotion.
- Understand how to answer appeals questions in the exam.

Common problems

Students tend to confuse appeal to tradition and appeal to history.

Students in exams tend to write, 'this is an appeal, so it is weak,' rather than really explaining why it is weak and why it fails to support the conclusion.

Strategies

Emphasise the following repeatedly.

- An appeal to tradition is an attempt to justify an action or a belief on the basis of long-standing practice or tradition – fox hunting is a traditional practice so it should be allowed to continue. However, just because something is traditional does not make it right. The rightness should be judged on its merits.
- An appeal to history is an attempt to support a prediction on the basis of past happenings or experience. However, the past is not a completely reliable guide to the future – just because something has happened before does not necessarily mean that it will happen again.

Give students plenty of practice at writing explanations of how an appeal weakens a specific argument.

Suggested activities

Worksheet activities

Worksheet 10.1 could be used in a number of ways. It could be used as a quick and simple matching activity, in which students match the examples of appeals to the names and explanations of what is wrong.

Alternatively, photocopy the worksheet and slice it into strips with one box per strip. Hand each student (or pair of students) one strip. Students must find those with the strips that belong with theirs.

Or, photocopy and cut up one sheet per pair, so that students can place the strips face down and play pairs.

One further possibility if you have more able students or very little time, would be to give them only the examples of appeals, and ask them to name and explain what is wrong with them.

Student activity

Ask students to read the tabloids, glossy magazines or a middle-of-the-road newspaper such as *The Daily Mail*. (Appeals can also be found in newspapers such as *The Guardian* or *The Telegraph*, but they can be harder for weaker students to spot.) Tell them to find and bring in examples of weak appeals used in articles or comment pieces. Give points to students or groups who produce particularly useful examples. Collect and photocopy these pieces.

Ask students to produce a display that includes the following:

- several examples of appeals in newspaper articles
- clear names of the appeals
- explanations of why the appeal is weak and the reasoning thus unlikely to support the conclusion.

This activity will give students the opportunity to read the papers, thus familiarising themselves with current affairs and debates and improving their language and their ability to engage in topical debate. It also uses their creative imaginations, which can help to internalise the concepts, and kinaesthetic and visual learning styles. It is also advantageous to have attractive, visual, subject-relevant stimuli in the classroom to reinforce learning and make students feel that Critical Thinking is part of the learning environment. It can be a problem if lessons are in a classroom normally used by another subject and Critical Thinking is marginalised in terms of visual display.

Guidance to worksheet activities

10.1 Foundation

1. c) iv)
2. e) v)
3. d) i)
4. a) ii)
5. b) iii)

10.1 Foundation

1. For years we have watched helplessly as an alliance of feminists, gay rights activists, divorce lawyers and cultural Marxists have attacked and undermined the traditional family, knowing that this was the surest way to destroy Western society. We must stick to our moral values and defeat this evil!

2. People want to know about celebrities' private lives, so papers should continue to publish stories about them.

3. We should invest in research in Tibetan people's blood chemistry. According to American psychologist Graham Peak, Tibetans have more than double the blood flow of Americans under comparable conditions. This means we could improve people's health.

4. Every time I've been out with someone, I've found them really irritating after about a week. I'm unlikely ever to find someone I enjoy being with long term.

5. Of course you should go to boarding school. Every first born male in the family has been to boarding school, all the way back to 1839.

a) This is an appeal to history, which refers to past events to justify a prediction about the future.

b) This is an appeal to tradition, which justifies an action on the basis that it is traditional without looking at whether it is right.

c) This is an appeal to emotion, which makes us feel emotional about an issue to get us to accept a claim rather than supporting the claim with good reasons.

OCR AS Critical Thinking

10 Evaluating reasoning: appeals

10.1 Foundation

> **d)** This is an appeal to irrelevant authority.

> **e)** This is an appeal to popularity, which justifies a course of action by people being in favour of it.

> **i)** A psychologist is not the best expert to use to talk about blood chemistry, so we should be cautious about accepting the conclusion. There is also no clear evidence to suggest how having greater blood flow could improve people's health so we would have to accept the conclusion *only* on the basis of the irrelevant authority.

> **ii)** The past is not necessarily a reliable guide to the future. Just because I have found previous dates irritating does not mean that, at some point in the future, I won't meet someone who does not irritate me.

> **iii)** Just because something is traditional does not mean it is right. Sending all those first born males to boarding school may have been cruel. Or it may have been the right thing for them, but the wrong thing for you. So we should not accept the conclusion that you should go to boarding school merely on the basis of tradition.

> **iv)** The author twists language to make us feel afraid of groups of 'others' and their unspecific but scary effects on us. This is not a good basis for accepting the claim that we must stick to our moral values.

> **v)** Just because publishing celebrities' private lives is popular does not mean it is right. Even those in the public eye may have the right to privacy. Arguments about this should be based on reason rather than popularity and nosiness.

11 Evaluating reasoning: flaws

CHAPTER OVERVIEW

In this chapter students will continue to evaluate arguments. They will learn to identify flaws in reasoning and explain why these patterns of reasoning do not support a given conclusion.

Evaluating flaws

Evaluation is the skill of judging whether an argument is strong or weak. In the case of flaws, evaluation is the skill of recognising key patterns of reasoning which give very weak support to a conclusion, and explaining why that support is weak.

Flaws

Student Book Chapter 11 pages 176–193
Specification 3.2.2

Learning objectives:

- Name common flaws in reasoning
- Describe common flaws in reasoning
- Explain why these flaws do not support a conclusion in a specific argument.

Common Problems

Students can barely do this at all. Many seem not to know what a flaw is while those who do tend to mix them up.

Many students try to criticise an argument by disagreeing with the reasons or by giving counter-arguments. Few identify the flaw and explain why this pattern of reasoning does not support the conclusion.

Strategies

Reinforce an understanding that a flaw is a pattern of reasoning that does not support a conclusion.

Remind students that they are not disagreeing with reasons or providing counter-argument at this stage but explaining why a pattern of reasoning does not give strong support to a conclusion.

Encourage students to read newspapers and bring in examples of reasoning that they think is problematic for classroom discussion. These could be made into a display.

Suggested activities

Lesson starters

Ask students to write down the names of as many flaws as they can remember at the beginning of a lesson. Ask for explanations from some students. Complete the list.

Start a lesson by describing a flaw, and asking students to name it. Ask a student to describe a flaw and elicit the name.

Put students into small groups to name and describe flaws.

Matching games

From Worksheet 11.1, the:

- names
- descriptions
- examples, and
- explanations

of what is wrong with flawed reasoning can be used in a number of ways.

Photocopy and cut up the worksheet for every pair of students. Alternatively, ask students to cut it up before beginning the activity. This will give weaker students the opportunity to see some correctly matched pairs. Ask students to find the names, descriptions, examples and explanations which belong together. Students could lay the cards face down on the table and play pairs – with any two of the four possibilities counting.

Alternatively, you could give students just Table 2 and ask them to write their own descriptions and explanations.

If you move all the names of flaws down one box, and insert the last flaw in the first box, the second table works like dominoes. Students can arrange the dominoes in a circle. Give points to students who finish correctly.

If you delete the contents of some boxes, candidates can fill the gaps.

Flawed letter

Ask pairs or small groups of students to write a list of five flaws. Tell them they now have to write a letter to a well-known figure which includes those five flaws. The letter must be a weak argument to support a conclusion. Students may choose their own well-known figure and their own conclusion. They may treat this activity seriously or with humour, as long as they produce flawed reasoning (and write nothing offensive).

Ask students to email you their flawed letters, along with a list of the five flaws they think their letters contain. Print and photocopy all (or the best) and distribute them to the class.

Ask students to work in groups and identify the flaws in others' letters. Ask groups to lead the class when their letter is being discussed. Encourage them to elicit explanations of why the reasoning does not support the conclusion, as well as the name of the flaw.

Students could produce written work on one of the letters, naming and explaining the flaws in another group's letter.

Writing arguments

Students can benefit throughout the whole course from discussion and opportunities to develop their own reasoning. At this stage, it is worth asking them to check each other's arguments for flaws. Doing so can improve their own writing while also practising the evaluative skill of identifying flaws.

Guidance to worksheet activities

11.1 Core

1. g) v) G (Confusing necessary and sufficient conditions)
2. k) xi) A (Reasoning from wrong actions)
3. h) x) B (Conflation)
4. l) ii) J (Straw person)
5. f) iii) I (Attacking the arguer)
6. d) viii) D (Circular)
7. e) iv) H (Slippery slope)
8. a) ix) C (Restricting the options)
9. j) vii) E (Causal flaw)
10. e) i) K (Sweeping generalisation)
11. b) vi) F (Hasty generalisation)

11.2 Extension

1. Slippery slope: the loose links in this sequence of events are extreme, but treated as almost certain. In this case we should consider the possibility that a decision about genetic screening may lead to further decisions, one step at a time, until we reach an unacceptable point. However, that is not what this argument does. It leaps to the concept of perfect babies and not allowing people to breed, which is extreme. On this basis, we cannot accept the conclusion that it would have been better for the British couple to have been refused the right to test their embryos.

2. This question refers back to the introduction of principles in Chapter 8, and forwards to the evaluation of principles in Chapter 12. It also refers forwards to the use of principles in Unit 3. Candidates may find that this makes for an interesting discussion. Principles that may be helpful would include: it is wrong to kill (unsatisfactory embryos are killed); life is sacred; any child is a gift from God; we should strive to avoid pain; we should act in the interests of the majority; we should judge whether an act is right on the basis of its consequences.

5. Paragraph 1: Causal flaw: the author assumes that the government initiatives caused the drop in performance in maths. However, this drop may have been unrelated, or the product of a complicated series of causal links. So we cannot

accept that the drive for education has been an unqualified disaster.

Generalisation: the author generalises from a drop in international maths league tables to the government's whole education drive being an unqualified disaster. But one area of poor performance does not imply poor performance in all areas. It may be that literacy and science have improved dramatically, which would make the education drive at least partially successful. So we cannot accept that the drive for education has been an unqualified disaster.

Paragraph 2: Slippery slope: the jump from underperformance in one test and the inarticulacy of one government minister, to the decline of the country, is too great.

(Appeal to emotion. The rhetorical use of 'this once noble country' is designed to sway emotions rather than to use reason.)

Attacking the arguer (Ad hominem): the author is rude about the education minister rather than engaging with his arguments and policies. So this reasoning does not support the claim that the country is going to the dogs.

Paragraph 3: Straw person: the author misrepresents the government's intentions and aims at trying to make learning relevant, in order to dismiss them more easily. There is an important difference between intending to motivate young people by making them see the point of what they are learning and dumbing down by teaching only what students already know. So we cannot accept on the basis of this reasoning that the government has lowered its educational sights.

Restricting the options: the author offers only two options – a failed state system and home schooling. There are options in between, even if we ignore the fact that the author has not supported the claim that the state system has failed. There remain the options of independent schooling or education abroad, for example. So we cannot accept the need for home schooling on the basis of this reasoning.

6. The example of the BTec in English is weak because it conflates reading and reading fiction. But just because students may not have to read fiction does not mean that they will not have to read other forms of writing such as newspapers (to a high level). So it doesn't show that the government has abandoned all purpose in education. It is also not clear that the BTec will teach young people only what is 'relevant' to them. So we cannot take it as an example of teaching only what is 'relevant.'

11.1 Core

Table 1

1. An argument that assumes that a necessary condition is also sufficient, or that assumes that a sufficient condition must also be necessary.	g) Working hard and having the right qualifications for the job may well be necessary conditions for getting the job. This doesn't mean that they will be sufficient, as there may be someone even more hard working, or with a more appropriate personality, or who bonds better with the team. So we cannot be sure that Refi will get the job.
2. An attempt to justify one (possibly wrong) action on the basis that someone else is doing it.	k) In this case, you can't justify damaging property as an expression of protest in the UK just on the basis that it has happened in France. If it was wrong for the French youth to behave like this, it would be wrong for us.
3. Bringing two or more different concepts together and treating them as the same thing.	h) This argument treats football fans and violent hooligans as the same, even though many football fans are not violent. So we can't accept the conclusion.
4. This flaw misrepresents or distorts an opposing view in order to dismiss it.	i) The college's reasons for not allowing a party in the summer holidays are being misrepresented to make it easier to dismiss them. Not wanting to take the safety risk of an unattended party is quite a strong reason not to allow the party, and is very different from being a killjoy.
5. A form of reasoning that dismisses an opposing view by attacking the person putting forward that view rather than addressing their reasoning.	f) College management is being attacked instead of their arguments being addressed.
6. An argument in which one of the reasons is the same as the conclusion *or* an argument in which you have to assume that the conclusion is right in order for the reasons to make sense.	d) The only reason given for darts not to become an Olympic sport is that it is not already recognised as an Olympic sport. But what is in question is precisely whether the Olympic committee should recognise it as an Olympic sport.
7. Reasons from one possibility, through a series of events, which are not properly, logically linked, to an extreme consequence.	c) Ceasing to sell alcohol to the under 25s is unlikely to have significant negative consequences and the chain of events that is predicted is illogical and extreme. We cannot therefore accept the conclusion that we would all be worse off.

11 Evaluating reasoning: flaws

11.1 Core

8. Presents a limited picture of choices available in a situation in order to support one particular option.	a) This ignores the many options between requiring women to live like nuns and accepting abortion, such as using contraception, or activities that might be unacceptable for nuns but which do not lead to pregnancy. So we cannot accept the conclusion that we should accept abortion on the basis of this reasoning.
9. Reasoning that assumes a causal connection without good reason, oversimplifies causal relationships or confuses cause and effect.	j) Just because the Internet has developed at the same time as exam cheating has become prevalent, does not mean that the Internet is the main cause of cheating. It may well be that the causes of cheating are coursework and the pressure to do well, and the Internet has merely made this possible.
10. A generalisation that moves from some or many to all, creating a stereotype. It may sometimes move back to one individual again.	e) Just because many girls may be more interested in shoes than politics doesn't mean that all of them are, and Dawn may be a girl who is more interested in politics than shoes. So we can't accept the conclusion that Dawn must be more interested in shoes.
11. Draws a general conclusion from insufficient evidence.	b) It is not reasonable to move from one chemical, which has some negative effects, to all chemicals being too dangerous to use in cosmetics.

Table 2

i) Sweeping generalisation	K) Dawn is a girl, so she will be more interested in shoes than politics.
ii) Straw person	J) The college authorities won't let us have a party in college during the holidays with no staff in attendance. They're killjoys. They just don't want us to have fun. We should go on strike.
iii) Attacking the arguer	I) College management say we should work really hard and perform well in the exam. But they're a load of idiots, so we can't trust what they say.

11.1 Core

iv) Slippery slope	H) The Government proposes to ban drinking for the under-25s. This would be the first step to disaster. Young people would riot, and do considerable damage to property, which would have a negative effect on the economy. This could lead to strikes and further economic downturn, which would mean that we were all less well off.
v) Confusing necessary and sufficient conditions	G) Refi is bound to get the job. She has all the qualifications they want, and she's worked hard.
vi) Hasty generalisation	F) Researchers have shown that ethyl benzoate, a common ingredient in shampoo, may cause itchy scalps and rashes. We should stop using chemicals in cosmetics, as they are clearly too dangerous.
vii) Oversimplifying causal relationships	E) As more people have had access to the Internet, there has been a huge rise in cheating in A Levels. If we get rid of the Internet, cheating will end.
viii) Circular argument	D) Darts should not become an Olympic sport. Olympic sports are determined by the Olympic committee. This committee does not recognise darts as a sport.
ix) Restricting the options	C) Either we require women to live like nuns, or we accept the necessity of abortion. We should clearly, therefore, accept the necessity of abortion.
x) Conflation	B) Violence and hooliganism amongst supporters after football matches is a real problem. All football fans should therefore be stopped from travelling to away matches.
xi) Reasoning from wrong actions	A) We should burn cars and buildings to show the government how unhappy we are. That's what young people in France have been doing.

11 Evaluating reasoning: flaws

OCR AS Critical Thinking

11.2 Extension

Read the passage below and answer the questions that follow.

> A British couple have won the right to test embryos for a gene that leads to high cholesterol levels and an increased risk of heart attack. This is a worrying step, as cholesterol levels and heart conditions can be influenced by diet and lifestyle not just by genes. It is but a short step from genetic selection of embryos in circumstances in which lifestyle is as important as genes to designing babies according to a wish list, and from there to allowing only babies which are perfect to be born. It would have been better for the British couple to have been refused the right to test their embryos.

1. Name the flaw in the passage above. Explain why this flaw means that the reasoning does not support the conclusion.

2. What principles might help to make a decision about such genetic screening?

3. Write an argument to support or challenge the claim that, 'Screening embryos for genes linked to illnesses that can be regulated by lifestyle should not be allowed in this country'.

4. Swap arguments with a partner. Check your partner's work for flaws. Consider how to rewrite the arguments to avoid any flaws you find.

Read the passage below and answer the questions that follow.

> The Labour Government in the 1990s and early twenty-first century put education at the top of their agenda. They wasted millions of pounds of taxpayers' money in developing a new National Curriculum and new standards and SATs. As a result, in 2007, international studies placed British students 24th in maths performance, down from 5th. This drive for education has clearly been an unqualified disaster.
>
> The underperformance of British students in international tests is just the first step in a long-term decline of this once noble country. The current education minister is a fitting example of what his own education system produces – inarticulate, fake human beings with fake accents and fake knowledge. This is clear evidence that the country is going to the dogs.
>
> Furthermore, the government has lowered its educational sights. It has abandoned all purpose in education, and aims to teach children only what is 'relevant' to them – i.e. what they already know. The new BTec in English, for example, doesn't even require children to be able to read at all. It will be possible to gain the highest marks without reading a single poem, novel or play. As the state education system is unworkable, we parents clearly have only one alternative: we must home school our children.

5. Name six flaws in this argument. Explain why they do not support the reasoning.

6. Explain why the use of the example of the BTec in English is weak.

12 Evaluating reasoning: analogies, hypothetical reasoning and principles

CHAPTER OVERVIEW

In this chapter students will develop and extend their evaluative skills. They will learn how to evaluate the use of analogies, hypothetical reasoning and principles in argument.

Evaluating reasoning

This chapter extends evaluation to three more complex forms of reasoning. These skills tend to differentiate between the most able and as such, it is recommended that students should master the skills covered in Chapters 9–11 before approaching this chapter.

Evaluating analogies, hypothetical reasoning and principles

Student Book Chapter 12 pages 194–211
Specification 3.2.2

Learning objectives
- Evaluate analogies.
- Evaluate hypothetical reasoning.
- Evaluate the use of principles in argument.

Common problems
Students tend to leave questions about these areas of evaluation blank, possibly because they are not sure what analogies, hypothetical reasoning and principles are, or have not made the link between the work they are doing and the name of the kind of reasoning.

Where candidates do attempt questions on analogies, hypothetical reasoning and principles they tend to be too vague and approximate rather than precise.

Strategies
Repetition of key terms.

Practise working with these forms of reasoning.

Ensure that students clearly understand that they are working on analogies, hypothetical reasoning or principles.

Focus on exam requirements to ensure that students understand the task and the kinds of answer they should give.

Suggested activities

Analogies: whole class work
Display the following analogy.

Requiring websites such as YouTube to be shut down because they are used to bully students and teachers is as intelligent as demanding that schools be closed because bullying takes place in schools.

Ask students what conclusion is being supported. They should suggest two closely related conclusions: 'it would be unintelligent to close down YouTube' and therefore, 'we should not close down YouTube'.

Ask students what reason is given to support this conclusion. The reason given is that to do so would be 'as intelligent as demanding that schools be closed because bullying takes place in schools'. This form of reasoning works by comparing two situations and implying that we can draw the same conclusion about them.

Ask students to:
- identify precisely the situations being compared
- consider significant similarities between the two situations
- consider significant differences between the two situations
- evaluate whether the analogy is strong, i.e. whether the situations are sufficiently similar to reason

about them in the same way, or whether the differences are too great to reason about the situations in the same way
- evaluate whether the analogy supports the student's conclusion.

Elicit ideas for improvement – or better analogies.

Students often use analogies in their own reasoning. When they do, highlight that the student has used a fairly sophisticated form of reasoning, and write it up. Go through the steps used in evaluating analogy, as outlined above.

For all three skills, it is advisable to work carefully through the activities in the worksheets and student book, and encourage students to follow the patterns of answers provided. Mark schemes and examiners' reports often also provide useful hints and tips.

Hypothetical reasoning: whole class work

Display the first part of a hypothetical claim such as, 'If the age of consent were lowered' or, 'If petrol cost £5 a litre'. Ask for suggested consequences and write them up. Elicit from students which of these consequences are most likely to follow from the condition (the 'if' clause). Consider what further conclusions could be drawn from this reasoning. For example, you may elicit hypothetical reasoning such as, 'If the age of consent were lowered, teenagers would feel pressure to have sexual intercourse at an even earlier age'. A further conclusion that could be drawn from this would be that, 'It might therefore be unwise to lower the age of consent'.

Principles: whole class work

Principles provoke discussions that really stretch students.

Display the following situation.

Housemates Tom and Aimee cook dinner for some friends during their first term at university. Their cooking is disastrous. Their guests manage to eat the food. Tom asks one guest, Serena, whether she enjoyed the meal. Should Serena lie?

Allow students to discuss whether Serena should lie. Write up any principles used by students in the course of discussion and highlight that they are using a principle. Suggest the following principles to stimulate or extend the discussion.

- You should always tell the truth.
- It is justifiable to lie in order to avoid hurting someone's feelings.
- Act so as to cause the greatest good to the greatest number.
- Do to others as you would want them to do to you.

Group activity

Ask students to work in small groups to discuss the principles above (or elicited in discussion) considering specific situations to which they do or do not apply. Students might also discuss how they might limit the principles. For example, it would be possible to limit the first principle to, 'You should always tell the truth if doing so will not have negative consequences'.

Guidance to worksheet activities

12.1 Extension

You may wish also to ask students questions about the use of evidence and examples in the passage. Students may also like to write an argument to support or challenge the principle that, 'Society has a duty to protect children from harm'.

1. We should resist the temptation to give in to the demands of these campaigners.

2. It is ridiculous to remove magnetic toys from the shelves.

3. Society has a duty to protect children from harm.

4. Children are not allowed to buy harmful substances such as alcohol, cigarettes, solvents, etc.

5. The principle provides some support for the campaigners' claim that the toys should be removed from the shelves but not a lot, because the principle is far too strong and overemphasises the role of society as opposed to parents. Society does not have a duty to protect children from *all* harm, although society may have a duty to intervene in *some* harmful circumstances. (It may be possible to argue this differently – credit acceptable, well-argued answers.)

6. If we leave these toys on sale, there will inevitably be more deaths.

7. This reason provides fairly weak support for the claim that we should remove these products from shop shelves. The consequence, that 'there will inevitably be more deaths' does not follow from the condition. It is possible that there will be more deaths, but it is also possible that manufacturers will change the toy, or put a warning on the box, or that parents will become aware of the dangers of eating magnets and prevent their children from doing so – either by warnings or by tidying up toys to keep them from younger siblings. In any case, a small number of deaths around the world is not necessarily a reason to cease to sell a product.

8. Parents should care properly for their children.

9. If we accept the claim that this toy is safe when played with appropriately, then the principle that parents should care properly for their children does seem to be applicable in this situation. The toy itself is not dangerous or faulty, it is the inappropriate behaviour. (Could be argued differently.)

10. Banning toys containing strong magnets because parents do not supervise their children is said to be unreasonable in the same way that it would be unreasonable to make the sale of toilet cleaner illegal just in case some parents forgot to tell their children not to drink it.

11. In both cases we would expect parents to exercise responsibility for their children's safety/in both cases serious harm could come to children.

12. It would not be unreasonable for parents to lock toilet cleaner completely away from children, whereas we would expect children to have easy access to toys; toilet cleaner is intended for adult use only, whereas toys are intended to be used by children and should therefore meet higher standards of safety than toilet cleaner.

13. The differences are probably not significant enough to make the analogy weak, although they do weaken it somewhat.

14. Even though the analogy is weakened, it does enough to support the conclusion to a certain extent.

12 Evaluating reasoning: analogies, hypothetical reasoning and principles   OCR AS Critical Thinking

12.1 Extension

Read the passage below, then complete tasks 1–14.

1. A growing group of campaigners are claiming that construction toys containing small, strong magnets should be removed from sale. They say that society has a duty to protect children from harm and, as around 100 children worldwide have been hospitalised with serious intestinal injuries from swallowing small, strong magnets, these toys are harmful. The oldest of these children was a 12-year-old American at summer camp, the youngest a toddler who found his sister's toys which had not been cleared away. The toddler, sadly, died of his injuries. The campaigners claim that if we leave these toys on sale, there will inevitably be more deaths.

2. However, it is ridiculous to remove magnetic toys from the shelves so we should resist the temptation to give in to the demands of these campaigners. Magnetic construction toys are safe when played with in an appropriate manner. No harm comes to a child who constructs three dimensional shapes from these magnetic components, takes them apart and builds something new.

3. These toys are, in fact, a fantastic, fun and educational way to spend time. They appeal to the whole family and encourage collaborative, whole-family play: girls, boys, grandparents and aunties. The dog may feel a bit left out, but will struggle to wag his way into trouble by sweeping the game parts across the room. Children can learn about magnetic attraction, maths and engineering, all without a single brain ache.

4. Parents should care properly for their children, and this means that they should supervise them and educate them about the consequences of inappropriate behaviour. We expect a parent to explain to a child that toys are for playing with and food is for eating. Not vice versa. Banning the sale of toys containing strong magnets because parents do not supervise their children would be as unreasonable as making the sale of toilet cleaner illegal in case some parent forgot to tell their child not to drink it.

1. Identify the main conclusion of the argument.

2. Identify the intermediate conclusion in the argument.

3. Identify the principle used by the campaigners against magnetic construction toys.

4. Suggest one specific situation in which this principle applies, other than removing toys from sale.

5. Does the principle provide strong support for the campaigners' conclusion? Explain your answer.

6. Identify the hypothetical reason in the first paragraph.

7. Does this reason provide strong support for the claim that we should remove magnetic construction toys from the shelves? Justify your answer.

12.1 Extension

8. Identify a principle used to support the main conclusion.

9. Does this principle provide strong support for the author's conclusion? Justify your answer.

10. Identify the situations being compared in the analogy in the last paragraph.

11. Explain one significant similarity between the two situations.

12. Explain one significant difference between the two situations.

13. Assess whether the analogy is strong overall, taking significant similarities and differences into account.

14. Does the analogy provide strong support for the author's conclusion?

Section 5 Developing Your Own Argument

Chapter 13	**Basic reasoning skills**	120
	Worksheet 13.1 Foundation	122
	Worksheet 13.2 Core	123
Chapter 14	**Writing an argument**	124
	Worksheet 14.1 Foundation	127
	Worksheet 14.2 Core	128
Chapter 15	**Developing your argument**	129
	Worksheet 15.1 Extension	132
Unit 2	**Guidance to the Activities**	133

13 Basic reasoning skills

CHAPTER OVERVIEW

In this chapter students will practise some basic reasoning skills, developing them from the rudiments they learnt in Unit 1. They will focus on giving explanations, but will consider also giving reasons, examples, evidence and suggesting principles.

Developing reasoning

Developing reasoning is above all about understanding the logical link which is required between the components of an argument. In this chapter students focus on developing the basic skills that will allow them to write strong arguments later. In particular, they concentrate on giving one component at a time and really making sure that there is a strong, logical, supporting link.

Basic skills

Student Book Chapter 13 pages 212–225
Specification 3.2.3

Learning objectives

- Be able to give a simple explanation or reason for why something might have happened.
- Be able to give an explanation that would fit in with the author's argument.
- Be able to suggest an alternative explanation to that presented by the author in the passage.
- Write a developed explanation.
- Know how to include evidence and examples to support your explanation.
- Be able to give a principle that would support the author's argument.

Common problems

Candidates tend to be vague rather than precise and focussed.

Candidates often have very poor language skills. Many scripts seem to hint at a candidate who can think but who cannot express that thought in writing. Marks can only be awarded to candidates who communicate their thought.

Strategies

Require precision. Use questions to make the student really think about the logical link between reason and conclusion or evidence and reason: 'Is that really a strong reason to support the conclusion?'

It is useful to start developing reasoning and using basic skills at the beginning of the course and allow students to develop their own reasoning skills in tandem with their evaluation skills. This should help them to apply their evaluative skills to their own reasoning.

Start with lots of oral and aural work, especially with candidates who have weak language skills.

Suggested activities

Whenever you come across an interesting debate, discussion or piece of information in the media, save it for a Critical Thinking lesson. Intersperse analysis and evaluation with discussion, debate and even conversations in which you push students to justify their opinions. Keep asking, 'Why?' and don't accept, 'I don't know' for an answer. Allow students time to think, but require some kind of response.

Radio and TV discussion programmes can be a useful way of developing students' language skills while also exposing them to a high level of debate and provoking thought.

The *New Scientist*'s 'Last word' section, and the books that have arisen from it, such as '*Why Don't Penguins' Feet Freeze*', are a good source of things to be explained and possible explanations.

13 Basic reasoning skills

Guidance to worksheet activities

There are many possible answers to Worksheets 13.1 and 13.2. You should judge students' work on its own merits rather than in comparison to the answers suggested below. In particular, you should focus on the logical links in students' reasoning. Ask questions such as, 'Is that really a rational reason to support the conclusion?' or 'What else would you need to accept for that to really support the conclusion?' or 'Is that a precise example of the situation?' or 'Is that really plausible?' Suggest that students use an Internet search to find genuine statistics for Q3 on Worksheet 13.1.

The following are examples of how the questions might be answered rather than an exhaustive list of possibilities.

13.1 Foundation

1. a) We want to read about what's going on in the world.
   b) I want to show Grandma how much she means to me.
   c) We want a holiday when it is not too hot and not too cold.
   d) Tom has terrible split ends.
2. a) For example, they have provided us all with green wheelie bins for recycling.
   b) For example, the 'Bright Sparks use Parks' project encourages young people to play football and other team games in city parks in the evenings, and provides mentors for young people with social problems. It hopes this will reduce the amount of anti-social behaviour.
   c) For example, a flight to New York from London can cost as little as £39.
   d) For example, Katie has connected to her inner feelings of frustration about the state of the world by learning to play the drums.
3. a) The British drink, on average, 2.5kg of tea per year per person, whereas other European countries do not even figure on the list of major tea drinking countries at www.tea.org.uk.
   b) The number of househusbands has increased by 83% since 1993, and over 200,000 men are full-time househusbands (in 2007).
   c) In 2006, 53.3% of boys gained 5 A*–C grade GCSEs, whereas 63.2% of girls achieved the same results. This is a typical difference.
   d) Women graduates earn £1000 per year less than male graduates within three years of leaving university.
4. a) I left my memory stick on my desk.
   b) Josh has broken his leg.
   c) Men are not naturally drab but, like peacocks, have a need to display their wealth and status. Sometimes they do this through their clothes.
   d) Men are more willing than women to engage in 'self-promotion' and ask for a pay rise.

13.2 Core

Sample answers are provided for 1. a) and 2. a).

1. a)

Students work harder these days than they used to because there are more opportunities for them. It has become socially normal for 16-year-olds from all sorts of backgrounds to study in the sixth form and then go on to university. So young people can see the point of working harder. There are also fewer jobs for people who do not have higher-level qualifications, so students have to work hard to get qualifications. A hundred years ago, it was possible to get a skilled manual job when you left school at 14 or 16. Today the economy needs university-educated IT professionals and bioscientists more than skilled crafts people.

2. a)

CCTV is not a good thing. This is because we are watched all the time and have lost our privacy. In addition to this, CCTV is useless for catching criminals because the images are too grainy to be used in court.

13.1 Foundation

1. **Give one reason to support each of the following claims.**

   a) We should buy a newspaper.

   b) I should go to Grandma's 75th birthday party.

   c) We should go abroad at Easter.

   d) Tom should cut his hair.

2. **Give one example to illustrate each of the following claims.**

   a) The council has a number of initiatives to encourage people to recycle more.

   b) There are a number of projects using sport or music to improve young people's life prospects.

   c) It is possible to get to America ridiculously cheaply.

   d) Teenagers find music an important way of exploring who they are.

3. **Give one piece of evidence to support each of the following claims.**

   a) The British drink the most tea of all the countries in Europe.

   b) Men these days are more willing to be househusbands than they used to be.

   c) Girls outperform boys in exams.

   d) Men earn more than women in similar jobs.

4. **Suggest a plausible explanation for each of the following.**

   a) I haven't got my homework with me.

   b) Josh is always late for lessons.

   c) Men's fashion goes through phases of being ornate and elaborate.

   d) Men earn more than women in similar jobs even though the women have better academic qualifications than the men.

13.2 Core

1. **Write developed explanations for the following.**

    a) Students work harder these days than they used to.

    b) Diamonds, emeralds, rubies, sapphires and pearls have been favourite gemstones in almost every culture in the world over the centuries.

    c) Many people put off work until the deadline is pressing.

    d) People are fatter than they were 100 years ago.

    e) Eating disorders are more prevalent in developed countries than in developing countries.

    f) Celebrity culture can have a negative effect on young people.

    g) 90% of Swedish people hug someone at least once a week. Only 4% of them hug their boss.

    h) Frost makes patterns on glass that look like ferns and leaves.

    i) Human excrement smells worse than cow or horse dung.

    j) Dogs eat cow dung.

    k) The average weight of a woman's handbag increased 38% between 2002 and 2007.

    l) A great many people have names that are associated with their jobs, such as Bob Flowerdew, the gardening journalist.

2. **Write arguments with two or three reasons and an example to support or challenge the following claims.**

    a) CCTV is a good thing.

    b) Father Christmas should swap his reindeer for a 4x4.

    c) We should not buy things on credit.

    d) We should make sure we have secure locks on the doors and windows in our house.

    e) Top football players should not swear at the referee.

14 Writing an argument

CHAPTER OVERVIEW

In this chapter students will practise writing basic arguments with a clear, simple structure and strong logical links between reasons and conclusion.

Developing reasoning

Developing reasoning is above all about understanding the logical link that is required between the components of an argument. In this chapter students focus on writing short arguments with a clear, simple structure, whilst keeping logical links tight. Arguments can become very complex, but at AS Level students should be able to master simple structures.

Writing arguments with a simple structure

Student Book Chapter 14 pages 226–243
Specification 3.2.3

Learning objectives

- Appreciate that writing your own arguments is just as important as criticising others.
- Understand the importance of clearly stating the conclusion of your argument.
- Be able to include several reasons to support your chosen conclusion.
- Be able to include an intermediate conclusion as part of writing a more developed argument.
- Be able to work to some common argument structures.
- Know how to include evidence and examples in your arguments.
- Know how to use counter-arguments and assertions in your own arguments.

Common problems

Students write their opinions or a list of points rather than an argument.

Students do not write down the conclusion.

Students write an argument that does not give strong logical support to the conclusion they have been asked to support.

Students try to write a balanced, even-handed discursive essay rather than an argument.

Strategies

Emphasise that arguments are essentially one-sided and practise supporting claims without even considering counter-argument.

Explain that essays, which are often required to be two-sided, use arguments, but that arguments themselves are not balanced.

Suggested activities

Breaking down the thinking process

Help students to break down the thinking process before they build up a structure. Display a claim such as: 'It would be better for students to go backpacking in their gap year rather than doing voluntary charity projects abroad.'

Draw four columns: Advantages of backpacking; Disadvantages of backpacking; Advantages of voluntary charity projects; Disadvantages of charity projects.

In groups, students should write ideas in each column. Collate them in the whole group. Ask students to research in groups to find some evidence and examples to support their reasons. They should find an Internet search for 'Voluntourism,' useful.

Discuss the issue, allowing students to express their ideas freely, even if they are not always expressed as

14 Writing an argument

argument. Prompt reasoning with questions such as: 'Why?' and 'So what?'; 'What can we conclude from that?'; 'What are the consequences of your ideas?'; 'How would you support that?'

When a student produces a particularly nice, concise piece of reasoning, it is worth interrupting the discussion to highlight it, write it up and analyse it to show the structure. Then return to the discussion.

Encourage students to disagree with each other and justify why. If you start early you can create a really fruitful atmosphere in which students realise that their opinions can be challenged without a threat to their identity. It should also help them realise that in Critical Thinking, it is not about the answers, it is about the fertile clash of ideas and the process of thinking.

Draw students' attention back to you, and display a template from Worksheet 14.1 with the conclusion filled in. Work backwards, filling in the intermediate conclusion next, then asking students for reasons that would support this intermediate conclusion, and evidence and examples that would support the reasons. Use some of the ideas collated in the four columns. Remind students that they do not have to agree with the conclusion; supporting it and agreeing with it are separable.

Ask students to write an argument to challenge the conclusion you have just supported. If you get one or two students to read their arguments out, you can give immediate feedback. 'Good, you've got two reasons supporting an intermediate conclusion, and the links of support are good. What sort of evidence could we use to support your first reason, do you think? Kamal, can you help?'

Structure

Every time you ask students to write an argument, remind them that they need the following.

- At least two reasons supported by evidence or examples.
- One or more intermediate conclusions.
- Main conclusion.

Give feedback specifically on the logical links and the focus on the main conclusion.

Evidence/examples

Ask students to research real evidence as often as possible. In the exam they will not be tested on their general knowledge and the examiner is unlikely to check the accuracy of the evidence. However, a candidate's argument, and the logical links between components are likely to be stronger if the candidate approximates some remembered evidence rather than inventing implausible evidence. Compare these two arguments.

Argument 1:

Research indicates that many women are concerned about their safety on the streets even in daylight, with fears of mugging highest. This indicates that women's safety is a real issue which needs to be addressed. We should consider whether CCTV might be one way of helping women to feel safer.

Argument 2:

A study by Professor Jameson at the University of London showed that 80% of women claimed to be scared of being mugged. This shows that women are not safe on the streets, so we should support safety measures such as CCTV.

Comparison:

The first of these short arguments is much more subtle than the second: the evidence is more plausible, and the logical links tighter. So it is best to encourage students to use real evidence in their arguments in class, and to approximate to remembered evidence in the exam, even though they will not necessarily be penalised in the Unit 2 exam for inventing evidence. In class, consider ways of approximating real evidence from students' research. Remind students of the difference between plausible and implausible evidence and explanations.

Practice

The more students practise developing arguments, the better they will become.

Guidance to worksheet activities

14.2 Core

1. a) This argument seems quite weak on first reading. It is poorly expressed. However, there is a structure;

the conclusion, although weakly expressed, is about right, and the reasons do give some support to the conclusion. We can analyse the argument as follows.

R1: Cosmetics encourage vanity.

Ex: (IC) Many teenagers won't go out without make-up because (R) they are so concerned with their appearance.

(Unsupported opinion): This is just vain.

Ev: Make-up can give you spots.

R: So it goes against what you really want anyway.

R: We have to kill plants to make them.

R: [We] pollute rivers with the chemicals.

IC: Cosmetics are also bad for the environment.

C: So teenagers shouldn't use them and we should discourage them.

This candidate has therefore done enough to get a low-medium middle band mark.

b) This is an excellent argument which suggests and responds to a counter-argument, has two reasons relating to hygiene, supported with evidence and examples, to support an intermediate conclusion, and a further developed reason as well to support the main conclusion, which is clearly stated near the beginning. There are no huge leaps in the reasoning, and there are close logical links between the components. High-top band mark.

c) This is a common type of response from very weak candidates. The poor candidate has tried to structure their argument, but has absolutely no understanding at all of how the logical links of support work and has randomly labelled sentences. The evidence is clearly invented and is irrelevant – it doesn't support the reasons. The reasons do not give us ground to accept the intermediate conclusions – although R1 and R2 might give us some reason to accept that cosmetics should be used in some circumstances. R3 would contradict the conclusion. R4 could be used in support of the conclusion, but hasn't been – the idea that we should use soap is unsupported, even though it is called IC. The candidate has used a conclusion that is much stronger than the claim they were supposed to support or challenge. This argument can access only low-bottom band marks.

14.1 Foundation

14 Writing an argument — OCR AS Critical Thinking

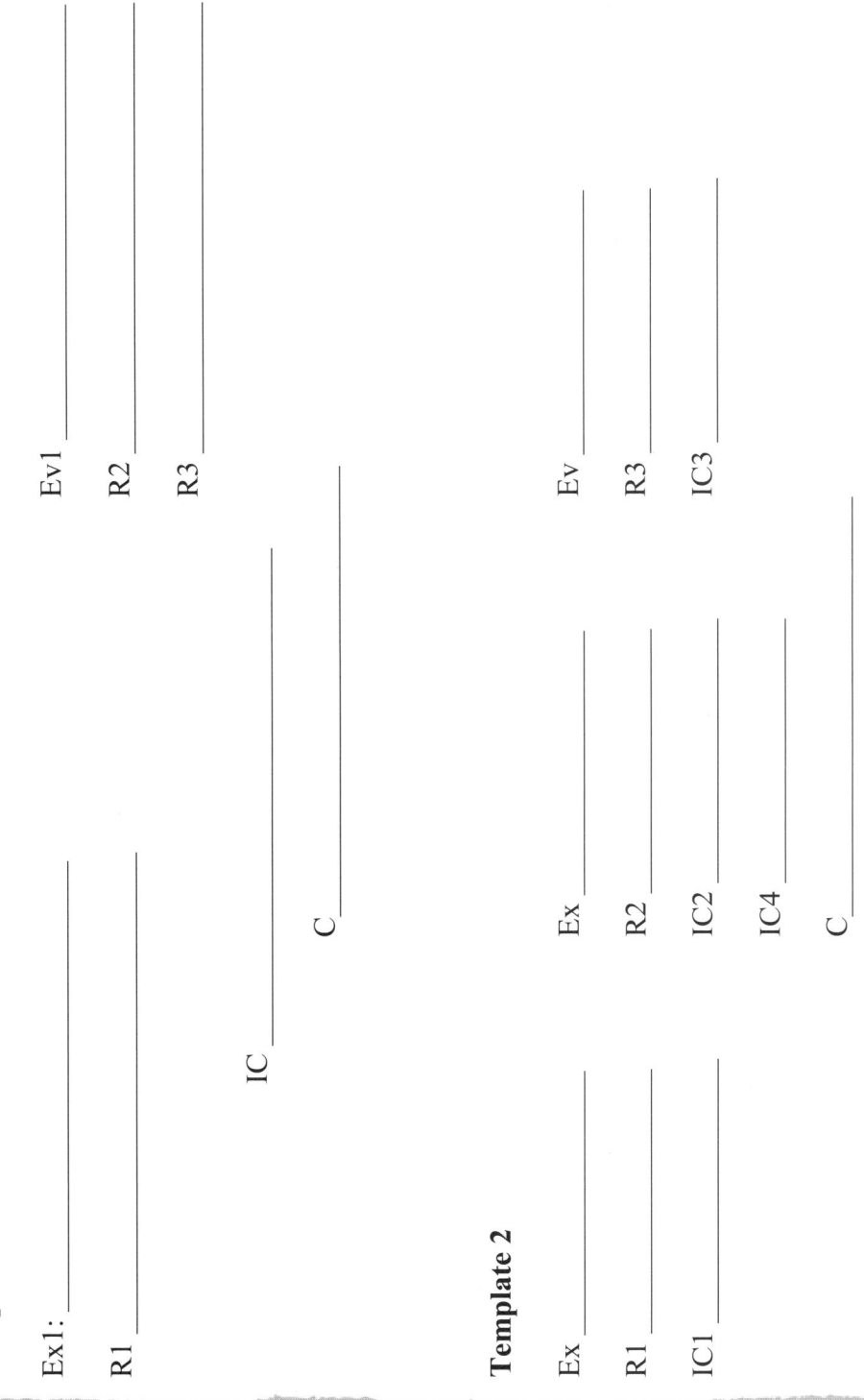

Template 1

Ex1: _____
R1 _____
Ev1 _____
R2 _____
R3 _____
IC _____
C _____

Template 2

Ex _____
R1 _____
IC1 _____
Ex _____
R2 _____
IC2 _____
Ev _____
R3 _____
IC3 _____
IC4 _____
C _____

14.2 Core

1. Using the mark grids from the most recent past papers, which can be found on the OCR website give a mark to each of the following arguments. Consider the structure, and the strength of the logical links. Candidates were asked to support or challenge the claim:

   'We should encourage the trend of young people not using cosmetics.'

   a) Cosmetics encourage vanity. For example, many teenagers won't go out without make-up because they are so concerned with their appearance. This is just vain. Make-up can give you spots, so it goes against what you really want anyway. Cosmetics are also bad for the environment because we have to kill plants to make them and pollute rivers with the chemicals. So teenagers shouldn't use them and we should discourage them.

   b) Although many people believe that it is better for young people not to use cosmetics because they can encourage self-image problems, we should not encourage young people to avoid cosmetics. First, cosmetics include soap, deodorant and shampoo, not just make-up. It would be really smelly in, for example, classrooms if young people did not use cosmetics at all, which would distract us from learning. Second, avoiding cosmetics might also contribute to the spread of disease, as washing your hands with soap is one of the best ways of killing the bacteria on them, for example after you have been to the toilet. Research indicates that poor hand-washing practice contributes to the spread of MRSA in hospitals. So there are many benefits to using cosmetics. Furthermore, we can counter suggestions that cosmetics are cruel to animals by making sure we use cosmetics that have not been tested on animals. The Body Shop, for example, sells make-up and toiletries which it does not test on animals.

   c) R1: Cosmetics can help people with facial scarring to live a normal life. Ev: 67% of people with facial scarring say they wouldn't go out without make-up. IC: Cosmetics are essential. R2: Wearing make-up can make it easier for shy people to go out into the world and be normal. IC: Make-up can act as a mask to hide the real you. Ex: You don't always want people at college to know what you are thinking. R3: Cosmetics pollute rivers with their chemicals. Ev: 89% of European rivers are full of chemicals. IC: Chemical pollution is a really bad thing. IC: So we should take action against chemical pollution. R4: Soap is a cosmetic. Ex: Pears Soap. IC: We should use soap. C: Cosmetics should be used.

2. Write arguments to support the following conclusions.

   a) We should discourage the wearing of jewellery.

   b) Man bags are the worst idea of the 21 Century.

   c) Schooling should not be compulsory after the age of 12.

15 Developing your argument

CHAPTER OVERVIEW

In this chapter students will develop and extend their skills in writing arguments, focusing on how to access the highest marks in the AS exam and taking their skills further towards A2.

Developing reasoning

Developing reasoning is above all about understanding the logical link that is required between the components of an argument. If candidates do not yet grasp how to write short arguments with reasons which support conclusions, most of the work in this chapter will not help them advance. This chapter is aimed at taking those who have mastered the core skills of writing and communicating argument further, to help them write more complex arguments.

Developing your argument

Student Book Chapter 15 pages 244–263
Specification 3.2.3

Learning objectives
- Avoiding weakness in your argument.
- Using counter-argument in your own arguments.
- Using hypothetical reasoning in your own arguments.
- Using principles in your own arguments.

Common problems
Writing interesting, insightful, perceptive and even humorous discourses rather than well-structured, strong arguments.

Including flaws, assumptions and irrelevant appeals in an argument.

Strategies
Sometimes you may have to be brutal with the most able students and give them a terrible mark to help them realise that the strategies which have been so successful for them in other subjects will not be successful in Critical Thinking. Require a great deal of these students in terms of sophistication and insight in class discussions, praise this, and help them to contain their ideas in a structure.

Suggested activities

Integration
Use students' own arguments for analysis and evaluation practice, to help them fully integrate the three assessed skills.

Stimulus
Provide students with newspaper articles or comment pieces to stimulate ideas. Discuss these ideas and continually push students to think one step further – to look at the next consequence, or defend their arguments against a counter-argument. Play Devil's advocate.

Counter-arguments
Display a claim. Ask students to consider reasons that might support or challenge it. Write ideas in columns. Ask students how they might challenge, answer or counter some of the reasons. Remind students that an argument is one sided. Including and responding to a counter-argument can strengthen an argument, but they are not trying to produce a balanced piece of writing. Counter-argument is included only to be refuted, not for evenness, balance or fairness.

Ask students to decide whether to support or challenge the claim. Tell them to pick just one idea from the other column, and think of the best way of answering it. They should include this as their counter-argument and response, then write a positive argument.

Guidance to worksheet activities

15.1 Extension

Students may respond to these questions in a variety of ways. Their answers should be marked using the levels-based mark schemes, with particular focus on the structure of their arguments. One sample answer has been given for each of the first four sections on the worksheet. This should be treated as one way of answering rather than as a restrictive model for how the question must be answered.

1. a) Use of and response to counter-argument.

(CA–C) Many people defend the current UK system of allowing 14-year-olds to choose whether to continue to study a language. (CA–R) They argue that students of that age can make mature decisions about what they need to learn. (RCA) However, (IC) 14-year-olds are not best placed to make decisions about whether to learn a language. (R1) At fourteen it is often more important to be cool than to be sensible, (IC) which leads to many young people making decisions they later regret, including giving up learning a language.

(R2 – hypothetical reasoning) If everyone learned a language until they were eighteen they would become competent speakers of that language. (IC) This would benefit the economy because (R3) many UK companies trade with companies in Europe and beyond. (Ev) Research indicates that a significant proportion of company bosses believe that they could make more money if they had staff who were competent in a language such as German or Japanese.

(R4) Learning a language well can also provide opportunities for work and travel abroad. (Ex) Learning Spanish, for example, means that you can communicate and work not just in the UK but also in Spain and South America. (IC) There are clearly many benefits to individuals and to the economy of everyone learning a language well. (C) So learning a foreign language should be compulsory until the age of eighteen.

2. a) Use of hypothetical reasoning.

(CA–C) Some people claim that there are circumstances in which it is acceptable to attack another country, even if that country has not attacked us. (CA–R) They say that it is acceptable to attack if that country poses a significant threat to us (Ex) if they might bomb us, for example. (RCA) However, (R1 – hypothetical) if we attacked other countries when they had not attacked us, there could be a much bigger conflict than if we had tried to negotiate a peaceful solution. (IC – hypothetical) It would also make the world generally more aggressive if everyone was prepared to attack in order to prevent other people attacking, (R2) because every country would be constantly ready to attack.

Furthermore, (R3 – hypothetical) if we attacked countries when they have not attacked us, we would be doing something both illegal and immoral. (Ev) International law states that it is an international crime to attack without provocation. (R4 – analogy used to support a principle) It is also just as wrong to attack another country in case they attack you, as it is to hit another child in the playground in case they hit you.

(IC) There are therefore, many disadvantages to attacking other countries if they have not attacked you, (C) so we should not attack in these circumstances.

3. a) Using a principle to support an argument.

(CA) It is often tempting to give money to beggars in the street, on the principle that we should be charitable and help those in need. However, (C) we should not give money to beggars in the street because (R1 – principle supporting argument) we should donate money where it will be most useful. (R2) Someone who is begging in the street is usually in dire need, and (R3) such need makes it harder for people to make sensible decisions about how to spend the money for the best outcome for them. (Ex) Drug addicts or the mentally ill, for example, will not necessarily spend the money in a way that will help them to find housing and work and a more stable life.

Furthermore, (R4) there are charitable organisations that provide shelter and help the homeless to put their lives back on track. (Ex) Shelter, for example, is one of many charities that provide real help to the homeless rather than just funding the spiral of decline that many such people have entered. (IC) It would therefore be

15 Developing your argument

better to donate money to such charities than to give it to beggars on the street.

4. a) Considering situations in which a principle might apply in order to support or challenge the principle.

There is a case for arguing that essential professionals should not go on strike, because the consequences can be serious. If firefighters do not put out fires, people might lose their homes or even die. If nurses refuse to care for people, some of them may die. If teachers refuse to enter the classroom, students will lose some of their education, and some may even be unsupervised.

However, it is precisely because the work of essential professionals such as teachers and nurses is so valuable and the consequences of them withdrawing their labour so great that these people should be allowed to fight for acceptable working conditions and pay. It is possible in the short term to draft in soldiers to put out fires, get medical staff from the army to cover a nurses' strike, or to organise child care during a teachers' strike. It would not be possible to run a good health care system or education system, if the nurses and teachers who want a decent standard of living left those professions because they were not allowed to fight for their standard of living.

Even essential professionals should, therefore, have the right to go on strike if their working conditions are unacceptable or if their employers, often the government, are abusing their dedication.

15.1 Extension

1. **Write arguments to support or challenge the following claims. Include a short counter-argument and respond to it.**

   a) Learning a foreign language should be compulsory until the age of eighteen.

   b) Teenagers are overprotected and spoilt.

   c) We've never had it so good.

2. **Use hypothetical reasoning to help you support or challenge the following claims.**

   a) We should not attack other countries if they have not attacked our country.

   b) People who are fourteen or fifteen should be legally able to consent to intercourse with those within two years of their own age.

   c) We should dismantle the National Health Service.

3. **Use principles to help you support these claims.**

   a) We should not give money to beggars in the street.

   b) We should respect our elders.

   c) We should buy only items that are ethically produced.

4. **Support or challenge the following principles by considering situations in which they might apply.**

   a) Essential professionals should not go on strike.

   b) We should donate a proportion of our income to charity on a regular basis.

   c) We should never go to war.

5. **Support or challenge the following claims. Use any strategies which seem appropriate. Remember to concentrate on the structure of your argument.**

   a) Freedom must be accompanied by responsibility.

   b) Reason is the slave of the passions.

   c) The point to life is enjoyment.

UNIT 2 — Guidance to the Activities

ACTIVITY 1

A 4 – an opinion.
B 2 – an explanation.
C 1 – an argument.

ACTIVITY 2

Passage 1   The answer is Conclusion C.

R1 Technology manufacturers would like us to live in digital homes where all appliances and audio-visual equipment are digitally controlled and connected.
E.g. Even our fridges will tell us when we need milk.
R2 Surveys show that most consumers want to use digital technology for no more than using the Internet or storing their holiday snaps on a computer.
C This shows that consumers do not want to live in a home with appliances that do everything for them.

Passage 2   The answer is Conclusion A.

R1 Health experts claim that GPs are prescribing far too many anti-depressants.
E.g. 1 People with only minor symptoms of depression are often given drugs when some form of counselling would be more appropriate and effective.
R2 The current availability of such counselling services is limited.
E.g. 2 With anything up to a six-month waiting list for NHS treatment.
C We should provide a much better level of counselling support at GP practices.
R3 Our GPs must be able to offer the best treatment to patients with symptoms of depression.

ACTIVITY 3

Passage A

IC More children should cycle to school.
MC The school should build bike sheds for pupils to keep their bikes.

Passage B

IC Passive smoking has negative health effects and is anti-social.
MC The government was right to introduce a law banning smoking in public places.

Passage C

IC This study underlines the importance of getting your five a day to stay healthy throughout life.
MC There should be incentives to encourage people to buy more fruit and vegetables.

OCR AS Critical Thinking   Unit 2 Guidance to the Activities

ACTIVITY 4

Passage A

CA Although many people enjoy drinking a coffee late at night…   R1 + R2
R1 Coffee contains caffeine, which is a stimulant.   ↓
R2 Taking any stimulant before going to bed stops you from sleeping soundly.   IC + R3
IC So drinking coffee before going to bed will stop you from sleeping soundly.   ↓
R3 A poor night's sleep may lead you to feeling tired in the morning.   C
C   Therefore drinking coffee before going to bed may cause you to feel tired in the morning.

Passage B

Heather and Bill have been living together for five years. **[An introduction to the argument.]**
R1 They plan to keep their relationship healthy by taking up new activities and interests…   R1 + R2
R2 as well as setting aside time to discuss their relationship.   ↓
IC They have in place good strategies to help them in the future.   IC + R3
R3 Many experts suggest that happy relationships rely on just these types of strategies.   ↓
C   It is therefore likely that Heather and Bill will continue to live together happily.   C

Passage C

R1 To stay healthy you are advised to have five portions of fresh fruit or vegetables   R1 + R2
    each day.   ↓
R2 You have only had four so far today.   IC + R3 + R4
IC So you should have a piece of fruit.   ↓
R3 We only have apples and oranges.   C
R4 And you do not like oranges.
C   So you should have an apple to maintain your good health.

Passage D

R1 The grass is very long.   R1
IC So we need to cut it today.   ↓
R2 We also need to go to town to buy food.   IC + R2 + R3 + R4
R3 It looks like it is going to rain soon.   ↓
R4 And we cannot cut wet grass.   C
C   Therefore we had better cut the grass before we go out to buy food.

ACTIVITY 5

Passage A. The correct answer is b) a conclusion, three reasons, counter-assertion, evidence.

R1 Fuel usage is a significant contributor to global warming.
R2 Increasing tax on fuel would lead to a decrease in fuel usage.
CA Although the government has suggested that people are not prepared to pay 'green taxes'…
R3 In fact people are willing to make serious changes to their lifestyles to combat global warming.
Ev In a recent study 83% of people said they were prepared to change their lifestyle.
C   Therefore the government should increase tax on fuel in an attempt to lessen the effects of global warming.

Passage B. The correct answer is a) a conclusion, two reasons, two examples, counter-assertion.

CA The introduction of the National Curriculum in 1988 was praised by many as it ensured that all students received a similar education.
R1 However, all children are different.
E.g. 1 Some excel at traditional academic subjects such as mathematics.
E.g. 2 While others are better focusing on more vocational studies, e.g. construction.
R2 The introduction of specialist schools has gone some way to redressing this balance in allowing schools to focus on particular areas.
C The Education Ministry should continue to allow schools to apply for specialist status.

Passage C. The correct answer is c) a conclusion, intermediate conclusion, two reasons, counter-assertion, evidence.

R1 The continued high level of divorce means that more people are living on their own.
EV Current statistics show that two in five marriages end in divorce.
R2 There has also been an increase in the number of people from Europe coming to live and work in the UK.
IC More houses need to be built to meet this need.
CA However, increases in house prices means that both buying and renting a house is becoming too expensive for many people.
C The housing built needs to be affordable.

ACTIVITY 6

Passage A I should walk the dog first (before it rains).

Passage B Girls care more about clothing than boys. Boys are more interested in hobbies than girls.

Passage C The population is ageing.

Passage D It would be better for me to buy a mobile phone with an integrated music player.

Passage E Conclusion 2.

Passage F Conclusion 3.

ACTIVITY 7

Passage A
Step 1
Expecting politicians to resist the temptation of gaining success by dishonest means is like leaving a very small child alone in a sweetshop and expecting them not to eat the sweets.

Step 2
We cannot expect politicians to be honest in the run-up to a general election.
(Students may find this analogy inadequate – and of course it is. You could refer forwards to Chapter 12 on evaluating analogy, or just ask them why the situations are not similar enough to draw the conclusion.)

Passage B
Step 1
The situation of not encouraging mature independent adults by continuing to spoon feed them past babyhood is compared to the situation of not encouraging the poorest countries in the world to develop

to maturity by not allowing them access to the means to develop their own maturity (the spoon of science and technology).

Step 2
Aid for developing countries must focus on the development of science and technology.

ACTIVITY 8

Passage A   Principle: We should not hurt them [animals]. Intermediate conclusion, supported by the reason that animals feel pain and giving support to the claim that we should all become vegetarians.

Passage B   Principle: It is not fair that genuinely ill people have to wait for treatment. Reason to support:
Principle: People who cause their own problems should not be treated on the NHS. Conclusion of argument.

Passage C   Principle: You should treat other people as you would want them to treat you. Conclusion of the argument.

ACTIVITY 9

D. This is a general recommendation that applies to many specific situations. The other three elements are either factual or specific.

ACTIVITY 10

a) Every child should have this opportunity [to learn a musical instrument].
b) Music clearly has a great many benefits.
c) Learning a musical instrument can improve their concentration.
d) We should do everything we can to aid children's education.
e) Depriving people of a musical outlet for their feelings would be bad for their health is compared with depriving them of medication to treat illness being bad for their health. (Students may wish to point out ways in which these situations are not analogous. This is not part of the analytical skill being tested here, but is a relevant evaluative skill, covered in Chapter 12.)

ACTIVITY 11

It is inconsistent to say that: 'We should encourage people not to use cosmetics because they are a means of concealing the true personality', and that, 'It would be better to use natural alternatives such as lemon juice or aloe vera'. If we should encourage people not to use cosmetics, this applies to natural alternatives to modern cosmetics as well.

ACTIVITY 12

a) Infliction of punishment on an offender.
b) For classroom discussion.

ACTIVITY 13

a) We should not expect improving the economy to improve the crime rate.
b) People are generally not responsible for their criminal actions.
c) There is a contradiction between 'People are generally not responsible for their criminal actions' and 'Each and every one of us is an independent person able to make our own choices.'
d) It is inconsistent to argue that we should not expect improving the economy to improve the crime rate and that people do commit crimes because of poverty/people will commit violent crimes because they feel alienated ... have so little. (Improving the economy such that these people were not poor or did not 'have so little' would surely improve the crime rate.) It is also inconsistent to argue that some of us are naturally criminal yet each of us can make our own choices.
e) Blaming Piers for his (criminal) actions would be unreasonable because they are the result of his genes in the same way as it would be unreasonable to blame Piers for the colour of his eyes because they are the result of his genes.
f) We should not blame people for things they cannot affect.

ACTIVITY 14

This argument uses evidence about the number of aluminium cans each person gets through to support a conclusion about reducing our consumption of fizzy drinks. As aluminium cans are used to contain alcoholic drinks and other liquids as well as fizzy drinks, and as fizzy drinks can be contained in glass or plastic bottles, the evidence is not precisely relevant to the conclusion. For example, if a person who normally drinks lemonade from plastic bottles switched to bottled water, this person would not be making a huge difference to the country's carbon footprint.

ACTIVITY 15

Answers may include the following. Each paragraph represents a very strong answer to an AS question asking about weakness.

Passage A
- The evidence is insufficient to support the conclusion because it talks about one competition for robotic, driverless cars held in America in October 2007 and uses this to support a conclusion about the safety of robotic, driverless cars in the near future. We would either need to know that this competition represented the very best robotic cars in the world, or we would need similar evidence about other robotic cars, such as Japanese models.
- The evidence talks only about the driverless, robotic cars and draws a conclusion that compares these cars with human drivers. To be really sufficient, we would need to have evidence about human drivers' performance on the same course in the same conditions.
- The argument moves from evidence that four out of eleven robotic cars succeeded in a test, to a conclusion about the safety of robotic cars in the future. However, the evidence is not sufficient to draw this conclusion, because we need to know more about the entrants: were they all the same or were they different?

Passage B
- The author's evidence about 85% of students at one college thinking it was good is not precisely relevant to the conclusion that the education authority should continue to close school sixth forms. The students at that college are not the same group as the people who will be affected. Nor are their opinions precisely relevant to education policy.

- The evidence is not relevant because of the timescale. The author uses evidence about one academic year to support a conclusion about ongoing policy. This is weak because that year may have been untypical.
- Evidence about the satisfaction of students at one college is not sufficient to support a conclusion about education policy. You would also need other evidence about this college, evidence about the other sixth form colleges, and evidence about the schools in the area to make a judgement about whether the education authority should continue to close school sixth forms in favour of sixth form colleges. A very specific piece of evidence like this cannot be used to support a very general claim. (See Chapter 11 of the Student Book.)

Passage C
- Evidence to demonstrate that Members of Parliament are not representing the views of the population has been used to support a weak conclusion: that we should lobby MPs for a new vote on this issue. This is precisely relevant, which is a strength, and it seems reasonable that MPs should vote again.
- The evidence is not sufficient to support the conclusion. If only 55% of the population would support this measure, then 45% would oppose it – and their views are being represented by MPs at the moment.
- We would need to know whether representing our views was the MPs' only task. If they are also supposed to make moral judgements on our behalf even if we disagree with them, then the evidence that they are not representing our views is not sufficient to support the conclusion that they should vote again on the death penalty.
- The evidence also suggests the MPs have reliably voted against the death penalty. It gives us no reason to suppose that they would do any differently this time, so supporting another vote may just be a waste of time. In order to fully support the conclusion that we should lobby for another vote, we would need some reason to believe that the result might be different.
- Furthermore, the poll is taken out of context; we do not know what the trend in opinion on this matter is over time. It may be that 55% represents the smallest proportion of the population ever to hold this opinion. It would be unreasonable to demand another vote on this matter if increasing numbers of people actually prefer the current situation. So we need more information about opinions to support this conclusion.

Passage D
- The evidence about cartoons watched on video or DVD is not precisely relevant to the conclusion that watching television contributes to sleep problems. Watching videos and DVDs is different to watching TV, and TV programmes may be different to DVD/video cartoons. It is certainly possible to watch TV without watching violent cartoons.
- The young children watching the cartoon movies may not be the same group of young children who have sleep disturbances, so the evidence may not support the author's reason.
- The evidence tells us that 62% of these cartoon movies contain images of injury caused by violence, but we do not know what percentage of children's viewing consists of these videos and DVDs and cartoons may only form a very small part of children's viewing.
- 62% is not a massive majority, especially as only half contain death; it is entirely possible that a significant number of children with nightmares are watching cartoons without images of violence and death.

ACTIVITY 16

The evidence about salaries and debts is used to support the claim that 'It is obvious that graduate salaries no longer match the crippling cost of getting a degree'. However, the evidence compares an average salary with a maximum debt. This is not a fair comparison: we should compare the average salary with the average debt – and even then it needs to be acknowledged that some people will have over average salaries and under average debts.

ACTIVITY 17

The evidence is relevant to the conclusion, but it is not sufficient. We would need to know exact numbers of tourists and, more significantly, which month July was being compared to.

ACTIVITY 18

Answers may include the following. Each paragraph represents a strong AS answer.

Passage A
- Silk is used as an example of a natural fibre. It is a natural fibre that is easily ruined, and other natural fibres such as wool and even linen can shrink and fade in the wash. However, silk is a particularly delicate and expensive natural fibre. Other natural fibres such as cotton can be more easily cared for. So it would be unfair to treat silk as completely representative of natural fibres.
- Neoprene is used as an example of a man-made fibre. It is widely used in watersports equipment and is, as suggested, effective. It is not, however, typical of the modern fabrics used in clothing, and it does require some care and attention to prevent it from smelling very badly and degrading. So neoprene is not, perhaps, a strong example of the benefits of modern fabrics.
- However, the examples in this argument do enough to illustrate that some natural fibres can be hard to care for, and that man-made fibres have some advantages that would support the conclusion that we should not reject modern fabrics out of hand.

Passage B
- Jeremy Clarkson using a car to race a marathon runner is an extreme example that does not represent the situation most of us are likely to find ourselves in. Marathon runners are unusually fit and fast, unlike the rest of us. The routes taken in Clarkson's race were also not direct. So this example does not strengthen the argument – even though there is reason to believe that it often is quicker to walk in London than to use a car.

Passage C
- The example of debates between American presidential candidates is an instance of an extremely important debate that has been won for superficial reasons rather than by strong argument. It is made slightly weaker because it is only implied that these are television debates rather than non-televised debates.
- It might be thought this is such an extreme example that it could not be said to represent a normal television debate, perhaps because the outcome is so important that participants will be tempted to use rhetorical, advertising and presentational tricks rather than developing their arguments.
- On the other hand, precisely because television allows them to use such tricks, this example shows that television can distort important debates.

Passage D
- Nowheresville Hospital is a strong example of a situation in which the introduction of strict new guidelines on hand washing has been followed by a reduction in serious infections. Because nothing else has been changed at the hospital, we are as sure as we can be that it is the hand washing that has led to a reduction in infections.

OCR AS Critical Thinking | Unit 2 Guidance to the Activities

- We can't be certain that the change in hygiene has led to the reduction in infections, but it is certainly plausible that it has contributed, and it fits with the evidence given.
- As an example, this is a clear illustration of a situation in which the proposed change seems to have had the desired result. As evidence it would clearly be insufficient, but examples play a slightly different role in argument.

ACTIVITY 19

One alternative explanation would be that more of us are getting these diseases because we are generally healthier and live longer, which gives these diseases time to develop – our ancestors didn't get them because they had died of something else (measles, infection, childbirth, etc.) at a relatively early age. However, there may well be other reasons, and it is probably worth discussing with the group whether our lifestyle may be a contributory cause.

ACTIVITY 20

a) The explanation seems quite plausible, but is unlikely to be more than one of many reasons underlying this link.

b) It may be that it is people who are naturally inclined to be aggressive who tend to play violent video games, so this is why studies find that people who play violent video games tend to be aggressive. (Accept other plausible explanations for the link.)

c) Evidence about violent video games is used to support a conclusion about video games generally, so it is not precisely relevant to the conclusion. Video games in general include brain training, scrabble, chess and other games that would be unlikely to lead to violence. The evidence is also not sufficient to show that parents shouldn't let their children play video games at all. It might be better to conclude that parents should limit or monitor how much time their children spend playing such games.

d) It is unclear whether violent gamers are people who play violent games or violent people who play video games, and this confusion weakens the evidence. If they are violent people, we cannot conclude that the games have turned them from normal people into violent ones. The evidence might be seen as insufficient to support this conclusion, because it shows only that people can see so many violent images that they no longer find them surprising or shocking. This does not mean that these people will then go on to commit violent acts.

e) The example of Harry is not particularly strong. The only strength in terms of supporting the main conclusion is that he does play car racing games, which are not very violent. This is the only suggestion in the whole passage that video games in general might have negative effects.
- Harry is a man rather than a child, so he is not relevant to the issue of whether parents should let their children play games.
- It is not at all clear that his gaming habits have changed since marriage, just his personality.
- It may well be that this change in personality can be explained by the fact that he no longer feels the need to charm Janey as he is now married to her.
- Janey's examples of Harry's violence and aggression are very minor. Kicking a shed door – possibly only to shut it? – and being grumpy are hardly signs of troubling violence.

Unit 2 Guidance to the Activities OCR AS Critical Thinking

ACTIVITY 21

Name: Appeal to authority.

Description: The author refers to the authority of the National Lottery Organiser to support their claim that 'There are psychological benefits to participating in the National Lottery'.

Evaluation:
- The National Lottery organiser has a vested interest in promoting the National Lottery as beneficial, so their evidence may not be objective.
- They are unlikely to have expertise in psychology, so this is just a layperson's opinion and not a relevant, expert authority.
- There is also no real evidence given, beyond opinion, to support the conclusion.
- The NLO's comment shows only that there are psychological benefits to winning money in the NL, not to participating generally. So this appeal does not strengthen the support for the conclusion.

ACTIVITY 22

Name: Appeal to popularity.

Description: The author refers to the popularity of horoscopes to support the claim that there must be some truth in them.

Evaluation: Just because horoscopes are popular does not mean that they must be accurate or truthful. It is possible for many people to be wrong. So this appeal does not give us a reason to accept the conclusion and is weak reasoning.

ACTIVITY 23

Name: Appeal to tradition.

Description: The author refers to the traditional smokiness of some English public venues and its place in British culture to support the conclusion that we should not disapprove of smoking in public places.

Evaluation: Just because smoky places are traditionally English does not mean that we should ignore the evidence and reasons that would support disapproval of smoking in public places. The traditions that are lost may be much less than the health (and perhaps new customs) that are gained. So this reasoning does not support the conclusion. This argument also generalises from two very specific public spaces to all public spaces (see Chapter 11).

ACTIVITY 24

Name: Appeal to history.

Description: The author refers to past events (the train never having been late before) to support a prediction about the future (it will be on time tonight, so I'll see you at the due time).

Evaluation: The reference to the past reliability of the train cannot ensure its future reliability. There may be leaves on the line, or the train may get stuck behind one that is slow moving, or the driver may not turn up for work. So this reasoning does not support the strong prediction in the conclusion that 'I'll see you at 6.30'. It would better support a weaker claim such as: 'I'll probably see you around 6.30'.

ACTIVITY 25

Name: Appeal to emotion.

Description: The author uses emotive language to arouse outrage and indignation to persuade people to agree with the conclusion rather than giving reasons.

Evaluation: Arousing emotion about money we have earned being 'squandered' does not show that the government was wrong to spend more on the NHS. It may be, for example, that pay rises and price increases were necessary rather than wasteful. So this is weak reasoning that does not support the conclusion.

ACTIVITY 26

Passage A 3. This is a clear appeal to popularity. It could also be seen as an appeal to authority (of the Prime Minister), but this wasn't on the list, because there can only be one right answer in a multiple-choice question. In a longer passage, and in real passages, it is possible that there might be more than one appeal or flaw.

Passage B 3. The argument appeals to the popularity of Trendies to support the conclusion that 'I need to get a Trendie'. But its popularity does not mean you need one.
   1 is a counter-assertion rather than an expression of a weak appeal.
   2 is a poor paraphrase of the passage.
   4 may be true, but does not express a weak appeal in the passage.

Passage C 4. The argument appeals to tradition, and 4 expresses this.
   1 is a counter-argument rather than the expression of a weak appeal.
   2 seems to be related to an appeal to (un)popularity but, again, is a counter-argument rather than an expression of a weak appeal in the passage.
   3 expresses an appeal to history, which is not what is happening in the passage.

ACTIVITY 27

a) Name: Appeal to emotion.
   Description: The author uses emotive language and an exaggerated account of the problems caused by lorries to make us feel afraid, angry and indignant, rather than persuading us by good reasons to oppose the trials of bigger lorries.
   Evaluation: The author has used emotion instead of reasons to persuade us and this gives very weak support to the conclusion. Just because bigger lorries might upset some of us does not mean that they should not be trialled.

b) Name: Appeal to history.
   Description: The author refers to past risk to support a prediction about future risk caused by lorries.
   Evaluation: The past is not a reliable guide to the future. Just because lorries have caused a risk in the past does not mean they certainly will in the future. The trials are a way of seeing whether bigger lorries will be risky. The author uses this appeal to history as a way of answering King's point about 'little risk' without evaluating King's evidence or responding to him. So it gives very weak support to the conclusion that the proposal to trial bigger lorries should be thrown out.

c) Name: Appeal to authority.
   Description: The author appeals to Philippa Edmunds to strengthen their argument that the proposal to trial heavier lorries should be thrown out.

Evaluation:
- Edmunds is from Freight on Rail, so her expertise is not quite in the right area, and she has a vested interest to represent road travel as dangerous, because that would increase the business available to rail transport. However, just because she has a vested interest does not mean that she is misrepresenting the dangers of heavy lorries.
- She gives evidence and reasoning that do actually support the claim that bigger lorries would be more dangerous, which would support the conclusion. So this appeal to authority has a little strength and does provide some support for the conclusion.

d) Name: Appeal to popularity.
Description: The author tries to use the unpopularity of bigger, heavier lorries to support the claim that the government should not trial such lorries.
Evaluation:
- Just because the proposal to trial bigger, heavier lorries is unpopular does not mean that it is not the right measure to take. There may be good reasons to support the use of bigger lorries that would outweigh their unpopularity.
- The government is supposed to represent the people, so it should listen to us. But it is also supposed to act in our best interests, which is not necessarily the same as what we want. So this appeal does not provide strong support to the conclusion.

ACTIVITY 28

a) Name: Reasoning from wrong actions (tu quoque).
Description: The author is justifying using illegal immigrants on the basis that other farmers and the catering industry are making similar decisions.
Evaluation: You can't use one bad action to justify another bad action. If it is wrong to exploit illegal workers, it is wrong however many people are doing it. So this reasoning is weak and does not support the conclusion.

b) Name: Reasoning from wrong actions (two wrongs don't make a right).
Description: The author is justifying the conclusion that it doesn't make sense for the government to try to stop us eating unhealthily on the basis that it doesn't try to stop us from skiing or tombstoning.
Evaluation: Just because the government doesn't try to stop some unhealthy activities is not a reason for it not to try to stop us engaging in other unhealthy activities. So this reasoning does not support the conclusion.

Take it further: here are some extra evaluative points you could make about this passage if you wanted to think more deeply. At AS you do not need to but you may enjoy the challenge.

The author is right to point out that the government is being somewhat inconsistent by responding in different ways to different activities. But this does not mean that it should not try to stop us eating unhealthily. Perhaps the government should put more effort into persuading us to behave sensibly with regard to skiing and jumping off cliffs. Alternatively, you might want to argue that skiing has health benefits as well as health disadvantages, so the government is right to respond in different ways to different activities.

The last point is quite an interesting one. It certainly supports the claim that the government 'controlling' our eating would be counter-productive. And you can certainly interpret 'try to stop us' as a form of control. So to this extent, it provides strong support for the conclusion. However, you could argue that 'try to stop us' could be a form of persuasion. It is not clear that persuasion would have the same

OCR AS Critical Thinking • Unit 2 Guidance to the Activities

contrary result. And it could be argued that it would be wrong for the government not to use its power and influence to persuade us to eat healthily, especially as unhealthy eating causes expense that the state (and taxpayers) have to fund. So to this extent, this line of reasoning would only weakly support the conclusion.

ACTIVITY 29

a) Name: Sweeping generalisation.
   Description: The author uses a stereotypical, sweeping generalisation that young men drive more aggressively than middle-aged women. To draw the conclusion that Amir must have been to blame for the accident (as he was driving aggressively). This is an example of an author generalising from the tendency of many young men to drive aggressively to *all* young men driving aggressively and then back to the individual.
   Evaluation: Just because young men generally drive more aggressively than older women does not mean that Amir was driving aggressively, or that he was to blame for the accident. Amir may not have been driving aggressively. If he did cause the accident, it may have been because he stalled or was too cautious. It may have been Susan who caused the accident – or it may simply have been an accident in which no one was to blame. So the reasoning does not support the conclusion.

b) Name: Hasty generalisation.
   Description: The author uses one experience to generalise that the café was terrible.
   Evaluation: One experience of a café is not enough to generalise that it is always terrible. The chef may have called in sick or there may have been a major argument in the kitchen. Either of these events could result in a café that is often good being terrible on one occasion. So this reasoning is insufficient to claim that the café was terrible and that the reviewers went to the wrong place.

Take it further: here are some extra evaluative points you could make about this passage if you wanted to think more deeply. At AS you do not need to but you may enjoy the challenge.
The author of this passage generalises from one experience to the café being terrible and uses this generalisation to support the claim that 'the reviewers seem to have been to the wrong place'. So the author is setting one bad experience against more than one (possibly several) good experiences. There is, therefore, more evidence that the café is good than that it is terrible.

On the other hand, it is likely that each of those reviewers only went to the café once and made their judgement on the basis of that one visit. This would be a generalisation that we would regard as weak. So we are actually comparing several positive generalisations with one negative generalisation.

We might appeal to the expertise of the reviewers; some of them presumably judge cafés and restaurants for a living and are quite good at making such judgements. This would strengthen their claim that the café is good and thus weaken the author of this argument's claims.

It is very easy for a café to be bad, and very hard for it to be good. So if you visit it once and it is good, it is not unreasonable to expect that a second visit might also be good, because the café owner and staff have done the hard work needed to make the café good. One bad experience can moderate the opinion that this is a very good café, but it cannot be enough to say that it is never a good café.

So, although this argument is not as simple as it first appears, the reasoning does not support the author's conclusion. It is probable that the café is not always terrible, and that the reviewers did visit that café and have nice meals.

Unit 2 Guidance to the Activities — OCR AS Critical Thinking

ACTIVITY 30

a) Name: Causal flaw – correlation not cause.
   Description: The author assumes that, because they first took a cold remedy, and after that the cold got better, the remedy caused the cold to go away.
   Evaluation: The author is assuming a causal link in a situation where there may only have been correlation. It may be that the cold would have gone away within a week of its own accord. They usually do. So the fact that the remedy was taken and then the cold got better is not sufficient to support the conclusion that the remedy worked.

b) Name: Causal flaw – oversimplifying causal relationships.
   Description: The author assumes that the cause of public unhappiness with GM crops is that they only benefit farmers.
   Evaluation: The author ignores other causes of public unhappiness with GM crops – the fear of unnatural things, the concern of unknown, un-researched effects, etc. So they have over-simplified, and it may take more than one of these causal factors to change to bring about an improvement in public perception of GM crops. So the conclusion is not well supported.

Take it further
On the other hand, self-interest is a powerful factor in perception of contentious issues. So benefits for consumers may outweigh the other causal reasons for the current unpopularity of GM crops. This would mean that there was some support for the conclusion, but the reasoning in the argument is still over-simplified and needs additional reasoning to strengthen it.

ACTIVITY 31

Passage A
Name: Confusing necessary and sufficient conditions.
Description: The author takes two necessary conditions for getting a job (qualifications and experience) and assumes that they are sufficient.
Evaluation: These conditions of qualification and experience may be necessary to get the job, but they are not sufficient. There may be many people who have the qualifications and experience to do the job, but only one of them can get it. So this reasoning does not support the conclusion that Kofi is bound to get the job.

Passage B
Name: Restricting the options/false dilemma.
Description: The author limits the options to just two: either dying their hair green today or never knowing what it felt like to express their true personality.
Evaluation: The author ignores other options, such as dying their hair green tomorrow, or finding other ways of expressing their true personality. So the conclusion that 'I have to dye my hair green today' is not supported.

Passage C
Name: Circular argument – begging the question.
Description: R If wizards didn't hide from muggles we would know the wizards were there.
C So of course there are wizards who hide from muggles.
The reason that we would know wizards were there if they didn't hide from muggles only supports the conclusion if the conclusion is true. But the whole point of a reason is that it gives us a reason to believe the conclusion.

Evaluation: The reason only supports the conclusion if we assume the conclusion is true. So it doesn't support the conclusion. It may be that there are no wizards to hide from us.

Take it further

Passage D
Name: Restricting the options.
Description: The author restricts the options to reintroducing wolves in fairly heavily populated areas or wolves becoming extinct.
Evaluation: The author ignores other options, such as introducing wolves to less heavily populated areas, which might be enough to ensure their survival. So this reasoning does not support the conclusion.

We also have to assume that reintroducing wolves to fairly heavily populated parts would be enough to prevent wolves from becoming extinct. It may be that wolves would not thrive in such areas anyway, and we would be increasing the threat of attacks without good reason. We would need more evidence to fully challenge this assumption, but it might be that this is a weak link in the author's reasoning.

Passage E
Name: Restricting the options.
Description: The author restricts the possible responses to the present crisis to all of us going to Lapland to help out or our children not getting any presents.

Name: Slippery slope.
Description: The author reasons from the first step of Father Christmas only having enough toys for half the good children, through a series of logically weak links, to the extreme consequence of an end to peace and joy on earth.

Name: Causal flaw – oversimplifying causal relationships.
Description: The author assumes that a lack of presents would cause a miserable Christmas.
Evaluation: Ignoring other options to the present crisis means that there is no support for all of us going to Lapland. This is further weakened by the overstated claim that 'our children won't get any presents'. They may get some. The slippery slope provides extremely weak reasoning and thus does not support the conclusion that we should go to Lapland. We may wish to argue that only really spoiled brats would allow a lack of presents to lead to a miserable Christmas – there are other things that contribute to a happy Christmas as well as presents. So this conclusion is thoroughly unsupported by this reasoning.

An everyday reaction to this argument might be that, 'Father Christmas doesn't exist, so it's rubbish'. This is, of course, the case. However, when we ask candidates to identify flaws in reasoning we are looking for problems with the pattern of reasoning rather than just disagreement with the reasons. It would be possible to write a sound argument based on the premise that Father Christmas had run out of presents.

Passage F
Name: Confusing necessary and sufficient conditions.
Description: Beauty is probably a necessary condition of make-up being successful for the cosmetics companies. However, the author assumes that it is also sufficient.
Evalution: It is likely that there are other factors as well as beauty necessary for a particular make-up to be a huge success, including not causing allergic reactions, being economically viable, being well marketed, etc. So, although it is likely that such make-up will be successful, the author's conclusion is too strong for the reasoning.

Unit 2 Guidance to the Activities   OCR AS Critical Thinking

ACTIVITY 32

Passage A
Name: Attacking the arguer.
Description: Mathilda Plume's argument is dismissed because of her vested interest rather than evaluated on its own merits.
Evaluation: Just because Plume has a vested interest to promote tobacco does not mean that her evidence is wrong. Her reasoning is not considered at all, so we cannot be sure that she is wrong, and the conclusion that the smoking death figures are accurate cannot be supported by this reasoning.

Passage B
Name: Conflation.
Description: The author treats unhappiness and mental ill health as the same thing.
Evaluation: The author conflates unhappiness and mental ill health but there are significant differences. Being depressed, for example, is a serious clinical condition, whereas being unhappy may pass by this afternoon. This means that we cannot accept the conclusion about taking happiness seriously, even if we ignore the further problem that unhappiness being expensive does not really support a conclusion about happiness.

Passage C
Name: Straw person.
Description: The author has taken a stereotype of some scientists as lacking social skills and not caring about moral values, and treated this as the reason that scientists are suggesting that computer games are good for children.
Evaluation: First of all, the stereotype is unfair and does not apply so it cannot be used to represent all scientists. Second, the scientists' real reasons for suggesting that computer games are good for children (that they improve mental agility, hand–eye co-ordination and problem-solving skills) are misrepresented so this does not give us a good reason to encourage children away from computer games. Third, the author uses an appeal to emotion, 'Those of us who value the truly important things in life', rather than good reasons. This means that there is no support at all in this argument for the conclusion that we should discourage children from computer games.

ACTIVITY 33

a) Name: Restricting the options.
   Description: The author restricts the option to either extending the retirement age or the British state collapsing.
   Evaluation: This is a particularly extreme pair of alternatives and leaves out a huge middle ground. There is no reason to suppose that even a bad pension crisis could cause the whole British state to collapse. So this reasoning does not give support to the conclusion.

b) Name: Appeal to emotion (specifically vanity).
   Description: The author appeals to the readers' emotions/vanity rather than giving good reasons to support the conclusion.
   Evaluation: This adds no support to the conclusion.

c) Name: Straw person.
   Description: Misrepresents the reasons for wanting to keep the current retirement age of 65.

OCR AS Critical Thinking   Unit 2 Guidance to the Activities

Evaluation: This knocks down an easy target but does not answer any real objections to extending the retirement age, so it does not support the author's conclusion.

Name: Attacking the arguer.
Description: Calls the proponents of a view 'selfish silvers' rather than engaging with their argument.
Evaluation: This is barely a flaw, and more of an insult, but it does not support the author's conclusion.

Name: Inconsistency.
Description: The author says that people who defend the current system are looking forward to retirement, yet also calls them 'selfish silvers', which implies they are already of retirement age.
Evaluation: This inconsistency does not strengthen the author's reasoning. But the reasoning was so weak anyway, that the inconsistency barely weakens it any further.

d) Name: Causal flaw – simplifying cause and effect.
Description: The author assumes that becoming ill is caused by having no interest in life and that having no interest in life is caused by having no job.
Evaluation: Neither of these causal relationships is as simple as the author suggests. So it is possible that some old people would be healthier if they were able to work – but as there are many reasons for lack of interest and many reasons for ill health, the author's conclusion does not follow. It may be that the reason people need to retire is ill health brought on by old age.

ACTIVITY 34

Passage A
Step 1
The situation of darts being a poor choice of Olympic sport because it involves no physical exertion is compared with reading being a poor choice of Olympic sport because it also involves no physical exertion – this reason is unstated.

Step 2
The conclusion being supported by the analogy is that we should not take seriously the proposal that darts should be an Olympic sport.

Step 3
Significant similarities: Neither darts nor reading requires the participant to be athletic or physically fit.

Step 4
Significant dissimilarities: Darts does require some physical skill, whereas reading is a mental skill.
Darts is competitive, whereas reading is usually not (you usually read alone, just for pleasure).
Darts can be interesting to spectators. Reading usually is not.

Step 5
But, reading is perhaps too extremely solitary and mental to be a strong analogy for a game such as darts. The analogy helps the reader consider what might make an Olympic sport, but the differences between darts and reading do mean that darts is a better spectator sport than reading.

Step 6
The analogy provides some support for the conclusion by highlighting how inappropriate it is to have unathletic events in the Olympics. However, this is not very strong support.

Passage B

Step 1
The situation of researching GM crops leading to damage which cannot be undone, is compared to the situation of setting off a nuclear bomb (to see what happens), which leads to damage that cannot be undone.

Step 2
The analogy is used to support the unstated conclusion that researching GM crops may not be wise (or close equivalent).

Step 3
Significant similarities: Both situations involve allowing bad consequences to come about in order to see just how bad they are.

Step 4
Significant differences: The scale of GM crops and a nuclear bomb are significantly different – the consequences of a nuclear bomb are considerably worse than those that might probably follow from GM research.

Step 5
The difference in scale outweighs the similarity of the situation, making this quite a weak analogy.

Step 6
Because the difference outweighs the similarity, the conclusion that researching GM crops might be unwise is only weakly supported.

Passage C

Step 1
Requiring journalists at film screenings to check their phones into a locker works (so that they cannot take pirate videos of the film), is compared to the situation of requiring 14 year-olds to check their phones into lockers before lessons would work (so that they cannot take videos of teachers and classmates).

Step 2
This analogy is used to support the conclusion that head teachers should require students to check phones into lockers before lessons.

Step 3
Significant similarities: In both cases the phone could be used to make an unacceptable recording so, it would make sense for individuals not to have phones.

Step 4
Significant differences: Journalists want to attend film screenings whereas many students do not want to attend lessons, so journalists are probably more likely to be willing to check their phones into lockers. Film screenings probably have better security and lower theft rates than many secondary schools, so journalists probably feel more secure about leaving their phones than many 14-year-olds do.

Step 5
The differences outweigh the similarities in terms of whether the measure would work. The similarities outweigh the differences in terms of whether the measure ought to be attempted.

Step 6
The analogy does not show that requiring 14-year-olds to check their phones into lockers would work. But it does provide some support for the claim that it should be attempted.

Passage D
Step 1
The dangers or negative consequences of building roads for car addicts is compared to the dangers or negative consequences of giving alcohol to an alcoholic.

Step 2
New road building can have a negative social impact.

Step 3
Similarities: Both addiction to alcohol and addiction to cars are bad for us. Addiction to alcohol has bad effects on the health and mental well-being of the addicted individual. Addiction to cars has bad effects on the health of the individual (who presumably walks less) and on the health of society (breathing fumes, not walking because of all the cars, getting run over, etc.).

Step 4
Differences: Alcohol is the cause of the addiction to alcohol, but roads are not the cause of our addiction to cars. A better analogy might be between building roads and building more pubs/off licences.
Giving alcohol to an alcoholic is immediate, involves intent and has a clear effect on a single user. Building roads provides infrastructure for those who just use cars rather than addicts, and is incidentally there for addicts.
Car addicts are different from alcohol addicts. It is probably not a physiological addiction.

Step 5
The differences outweigh the similarities in this analogy. There is an important similarity, but the analogy does not quite work.

Step 6
So we could not conclude that we should not build roads in the same way that we should not give alcohol to an alcoholic. However, the analogy does highlight the negative effects of road building, so it does give some support to the claim that 'new road building can have a negative social impact'.

Passage E
Step 1
Depriving people of a musical outlet for their feelings being bad for their health is compared with depriving them of medication to treat illness being bad for their health.

Step 2
The analogy is used to support the unstated conclusion that it would be wrong to deprive people of a musical outlet for their feelings, and (in the original passage in Chapter 8) this would support the claim that everyone should have the opportunity to learn a musical instrument.

Step 3
Similarities: If music keeps you feeling healthy and happy, and medication keeps you feeling healthy and happy, then depriving people of music would be similar to taking their medication away. Both would have negative effects on our health.

Step 4
Differences: The use of music is described in the paragraph as preventing possible mental ill health rather than curing it, and this is then compared with medication to cure ill health. So not using music wouldn't necessarily be as bad for their health.
Music is natural and free from side effects unlike medication, which can have side effects that make us feel ill. So in this respect, depriving people of music would be worse for their health than depriving them of medication.
There is an important difference between not providing an opportunity and taking medicine away.

Unit 2 Guidance to the Activities OCR AS Critical Thinking

Step 5
The analogy highlights an important issue about preventative health, and about mental vs physical health, and makes us consider whether not funding music lessons is as bad as not funding medical care. However, the differences outweigh the similarities.

Step 6
The analogy probably does enough to support the conclusion (that it would be wrong to deprive people of a musical outlet for their feelings) but only just. The conclusion needs the other support given in the paragraph.

ACTIVITY 35

Passage A
Is the condition likely? Many people do have unprotected sex, so the condition is not unlikely in general.

Does the consequence follow from the condition? The consequences are too strongly stated. They are expressed as a certainty. Having unprotected sex once may not lead to either of these consequences. However, both consequences are likely as a result of unprotected sex. Both consequences are also very serious and have long-lasting effects.

Does the hypothetical reasoning support the conclusion? Even though the consequences are too strongly stated, they are both likely and serious, so this does support the conclusion that you should use a condom.

Passage B
Is the condition likely? It is probably not likely in the near future that we will stop paying a licence fee, but the point is continually debated. It is plausible that it might be stopped.

Does the consequence follow from the condition? The BBC would have to find funding from somewhere if it wanted to continue broadcasting without income from the licence fee, and adverts would be an obvious answer. However, the options presented here may be restricted. It may be possible for the government to fund the BBC from general taxation, and this may have less effect on its status as a public service broadcaster than becoming commercial. However, state-run broadcasting tends to be less impartial than we would like the BBC to be.

Does the hypothetical reasoning support the conclusion? The reasoning gives some support to the conclusion. Despite the possible restriction of the options in the consequences, the argument does show that public service broadcasting (funded by a licence fee) is something we want to keep, and that this means we should keep the licence fee.

Passage C
Is the condition likely? It is highly likely that we want talented youngsters to work hard to excel at their sport. The looming London Olympics adds to this.

Does the consequence follow from the condition? This is quite a complicated piece of reasoning. It seems likely that praising people who achieve highly (but are not the best in the world) would encourage young people to work to excel. It seems likely (to me) that defining excellent and success to mean only 'coming first in the world' will be off-putting to many. On the other hand, it is possible that this will spur people on to better achievements, knowing that only the best is good enough. (It may be worth discussing this with the group. This last point can be seen as a highly damaging attitude.)

Does the hypothetical reasoning support the conclusion? Probably, but this depends on what we decide about the consequence following from the condition.

Passage D

This passage has several fairly unlikely conditions, draws some fairly implausible conclusions from the conditions and uses these to support a definite conclusion about what we should do now. This is very close to slippery slope reasoning.

Is the condition likely? 'If the lump of rock and metal hit us…'. It is fairly unlikely, although not impossible, that an asteroid predicted to come within 20,000 miles of Earth might hit us. More recent observations indicate that a collision is extremely unlikely. Comprehensible information can easily be found by using a search engine to look up Asteroid 2004 MN4.

Does the consequence follow from the condition? In this case, the consequence follows very clearly from the condition.

Does the hypothetical reasoning support the conclusion? The condition is so unlikely that, however certain the devastation if an asteroid hit us, spending money now to prepare for space tug development to avoid a collision seems extreme.

Are the conditions likely? The three possibilities for action are fairly unlikely. It is certainly not very plausible that we might be able to develop any of this technology. How would we cover an asteroid with aluminium foil?

Do the consequences follow from the conditions? None of the consequences seems likely to follow from the attempts.

Does the hypothetical reasoning support the conclusion? Nothing in this reasoning supports the strong conclusion that we should start preparing space tug development.

ACTIVITY 36

This activity should give rise to wide-ranging discussion. There are some situations to consider in each case.

A Obesity, anorexia, alcoholism, smoking, skiing or sports-related injuries, pregnancy, injuries sustained in fights, injuries sustained after accidents when you were speeding/not concentrating….
It might be worth raising the suggestion for discussion that some of these are conditions that need treatment rather than lifestyle choices. Obesity, for example, is widely regarded as the result of laziness, greed and poor lifestyle choices. However, it often has deep psychosocial roots and sometimes physical and genetic causes. It might make more sense to treat the underlying problems rather than bullying the obese and refusing them treatment for which they pay through their taxes.

B Drug addicts, shop lifters, fraudsters, tax avoiders…. Should any of these people receive NHS treatment? Should a drunk involved in a fight receive treatment for the broken nose?

C Even those who do not help themselves?

D Does a single mother on benefits who spends time talking to and playing with her kids and volunteers with the Samaritans contribute to society? Does a multi-millionaire banker with yacht and no social conscience contribute to society? Consider what 'contribute' and 'benefit' might mean. Do we mean only financially?

E What about people who refuse to work or those who disrupt others' education? Should juvenile criminals have a place in school? Adults who didn't make much of school as children?

Unit 2 Guidance to the Activities OCR AS Critical Thinking

ACTIVITY 37

Passage A
Principle: We should put the future of the world before our selfish desires.

How generally does the principle apply? This principle seems to apply fairly generally. However, the problem with this principle is that, if we followed it, we would never do anything at all. We would not be able to consume, build houses, turn the heating on, drive to work or college… . Indeed, to protect the world for the future, it would probably be best to significantly reduce the world's population and significantly reduce our standard of living. This comes into such great conflict with our need for self-preservation and self-betterment that we cannot act on it. So, if we cannot fully act on this principle, where do we draw the line? At what stage is our selfish self and species preservation to be overridden by the need to put the future of the world before our selfish desires?

Does the principle support the conclusion? Yes, the principle does give us grounds for moderating our lifestyle. But, because it is an open question where we draw the line, it is not a useful guide to action.

Passage B
Principle: It is not fair that genuinely ill people have to wait for treatment.

How generally does the principle apply? We certainly wouldn't feel that it was fair for a person who lived a healthy life but was having a heart attack to wait for treatment because A&E was too busy dealing with people who had been jumping off cliffs but had landed on submerged rocks. On the other hand, the use of 'genuinely ill' would imply that only those who have not inflicted damage on themselves are genuinely ill. Yet the person who eats too many fried eggs for breakfast is just as genuinely ill when they have a heart attack as the person who eats fruit for breakfast. The person who damages themselves more directly, perhaps by cutting their wrist, is genuinely ill and in need of treatment. Are smokers and drinkers different? This is an open question for discussion. Most of us would feel that, if two people had liver cirrhosis, one was an alcoholic and the other was not, the non-alcoholic should have priority for the liver transplant. On the other hand, it would seem very harsh to say: 'You have made some bad choices in your life. So you can't have access to health care.'

Does the principle support the conclusion? The conclusion is itself a principle. The first principle does not really support the conclusion that people who cause their own problems should not be treated in hospital.

Passage C
Principle: We should protect our common land.

How generally does the principle apply? In general, it does seem that we should protect our common land. However, would we want to protect this open space if most young people could not afford a home, or if people were living in unacceptably crowded conditions? Would our decision be altered if these 345 homes were for rich people or poor people?

Does the principle support the conclusion? Yes, if we accept that we should protect our common land, then we should accept the conclusion, because that is a specific measure to take to protect common land.

ACTIVITY 38

a) How likely is the condition? If aid were focused on developing Africa's science and technology base (and the thrust of the argument is that it should be), then it is plausible and probable that Africa could develop a science and technology base.

OCR AS Critical Thinking — Unit 2 Guidance to the Activities

Does the consequence follow from the condition? It is highly likely that African scientists, properly funded and working in Africa, would research diseases that affect African people. This would go some way towards redressing the current imbalance. One alternative consequence might be that more educated Africans would migrate, but it is probable that this would happen alongside research in Africa.

Does the reasoning support the conclusion? Yes.

b) Is the condition likely? It is a big step from focusing aid on the development of science and technology to Africa developing centres of excellence. It is plausible, and possible that this could happen. But there are many practical barriers to this condition.

Do the consequences follow from the condition? The consequences are too strongly stated. They may happen, but are not certain. Closing the scientific gap with the rest of the world is a big step; narrowing it would certainly happen. The best African scientists would still probably lack funding in comparison to scientists in richer countries, and this would make a difference. A skills base right across the educational system would take years or even generations to develop – but once that has happened, then the capacity to provide clean water will follow. It remains possible – and sadly, even likely – that there would be a division between those who are educated and those who are not.

Does the reasoning support the conclusion? Despite being overly optimistic and overstated, the reasoning does give some support to the conclusion. Some of the benefits are likely to come about, and providing aid that focuses on the development of science and technology is likely to have more benefit than aid that ships in western scientists. So this does give us grounds to believe that aid for developing nations should focus on science and technology.

c) It seems hard to think of a situation in which the principle that we have a duty to give aid that really aids does not apply. However, science and technology might not always aid (see answers to other questions), and there may be other forms of aid that are useful and genuinely aid. So the principle gives some but not very strong support to the conclusion.

d) The situation of not encouraging mature independent adults by continuing to spoon feed them beyond babyhood is compared to the situation of not encouraging the poorest countries in the world to develop to maturity by not allowing them access to the means to develop their own maturity (the spoon of science and technology).

e) The analogy specifically puts developing nations in the position of children and developed nations in the position of adults. This could be seen as patronising.

Similarities: The poorest countries are, to a certain extent, dependent on the richest. Allowing a child to make mistakes with a spoon will assist learning and development. Funding the development of science and technology in developing countries (giving them the spoon) will probably help them develop rather than remaining dependent.

Differences: The nature of the dependence of poor countries on rich countries is different from the adult–child relationship. The problem is that educated Africans need to come to the West to have access to spoons, and many Africans do not have access to suitable education because we have all the spoons. So the analogy would be better expressed as sharing our spoons fairly, rather than as an adult–child relationship.

The differences probably do not significantly outweigh the similarities. However we see the imagery, it remains the case that Africans need access to the spoon of science and technology. So the analogy gives fairly strong support to the claim that aid for developing nations must focus on the development of science and technology.

Unit 2 Guidance to the Activities OCR AS Critical Thinking

ACTIVITY 39

Below are some possible answers.

A Families rarely sit down together at the table and eat a meal together.
   - People prefer to eat with a tray watching the television.
   - Parents might do shift work.
   - Children are at sports clubs/music lessons/etc.
   - Microwaves have made it easier for each person to eat when they want.

B More students are choosing to go to university in their home town rather than a university further away.
   - It is cheaper to stay at home than pay for university accommodation.
   - Increased transport costs means it is cheaper not to study away from home.
   - Universities offer a wider range of courses than before so they are able to study their chosen course without moving.
   - There are now more universities so now most cities have at least one university.

C There has been an increase in the number of European holidays British people take each year.
   - Cheap cost of flights with 'no frills' airlines.
   - More regional airports means it is easier to fly abroad.
   - People are more wealthy so can afford to go away more often.
   - Travel programmes have increased people's interest in travelling to Europe.

ACTIVITY 40

A Here the author suggests that the reason why 'most electronic stores no longer sell VHS video recorders' is because it is very difficult to buy films on media other than DVD.
   Other possible explanations could be:
   - people use systems like Sky+ or on-demand services to watch their favourite programmes rather than recording them on video if they are busy
   - the quality of films on DVD is better than VHS video.

B Here the author suggests that the reason why 'people still prefer to drive [their cars] into the city' rather than take public transport is because 'we prefer the privacy of our own car to sharing transport with others'.
   Other possible explanations could be:
   - the place where they work/where they are going isn't near a public transport connection
   - they will be coming home after public transport has closed down
   - it costs them more to travel by public transport than by private car
   - it will take them longer
   - they would have to make several connections.

ACTIVITY 41

a) Explanations that would support the claim that the increased sales of organic food is a result of people's concern about food scares include:
   - people's concern about bird flu affecting chickens
   - people are concerned about eating genetically modified (GM) crops.

b) Alternative explanations for the increase in the sales of organic food could include:
   - people chose to buy organic food because they think it tastes better

- people buy organic food as it is better for the environment, it is produced without chemicals and pesticides
- organic fruit and vegetables can be delivered by box schemes from local producers; this reduces the amount of food miles
- people buy organic meat, because they want animals to be treated humanely before they are killed for food.

ACTIVITY 42

This question is looking for an understanding of the comparison between London and other areas of the country.

Possible answer supporting the idea that it would not have the same impact

The example of London might well be relevant to other crowded cities such as Birmingham or Bristol but is clearly not relevant to motorways or rural areas. The congestion charging scheme works well in London because there is a good public transport system, e.g. regular tubes and buses that mean people can get to places easily without taking their car. Or, places that people want to travel to are nearby so people can walk. People who live in villages don't have this option as there might not be a regular bus service and the nearest shops might be too far away to walk.

Possible answer supporting the idea that it would not have the same impact

Given that the congestion charging scheme has worked in London, a national road charging scheme will reduce congestion across the country. The scheme in London has proved that people are not prepared to pay an additional cost to travel by car at peak times and instead either take public transport or walk to where they want to go.

ACTIVITY 43

Possible answers

a)
A Parents who earn more than £60,000 a year shouldn't receive child benefit:
- wealthy parents shouldn't receive financial support from the government
- the government should only give financial support to those who need it/the government should allocate its resources to those who need it most
- money raised from taxes should not be given in benefits to those who don't need it.

B It was wrong for the police to plant evidence on the Great Train Robbers:
- the police should only use evidence gained without deception
- the police should operate within the law.

b)
Analysis of Passage C
R1   The New Eurostar station open at St Pancras in London.
IC1 You don't have to take the tube across London.
IC2 Reaching parts of Europe by train is much easier from parts of England than before.
R2   The check-in time for flying to Europe is longer than for travelling by train.
R3   Travelling by train will have less of an impact on the environment.
C   I think it is better to take the train from Birmingham to Paris rather than to fly.

Unit 2 Guidance to the Activities OCR AS Critical Thinking

The argument could be supported by the following general principles.
- We should travel in ways that cause least harm to the environment/we should travel in an environmentally friendly way.
- We should try to reduce our carbon footprint.
- We should think about the effect on the environment before we travel.

ACTIVITY 44

The following are just examples of possible answers. You may have chosen different reasons.

A It is my birthday and it is traditional to buy drinks for someone on their birthday. **[joint support – both are needed to support the conclusion]** Plus I haven't got any money on me! **[gives independent support for conclusion]**

B I have worked lots of extra hours. I have been covering the work of a more senior employee while they are away. **[independent support – either supports the conclusion]** I have also been on some relevant training courses to help me deal with this extra responsibility. **[gives joint support with the second reason]**

C My phone has all the latest features. It is very stylish and it was value for money when compared to similar models. **[all give independent support to the conclusion]**

D There are many opportunities for promotion and there is the chance to make a difference in young people's lives. You also receive a good pension when you retire. **[independent support]**

ACTIVITY 45

Both A and D are very strong conclusions in that they give us very specific outcomes. A suggests that clam shell phones are 'much better'. We could make this one weaker by saying that they have some advantages or that they are better in some situations. D suggests that reducing fat in our diet 'prevents' heart disease. We are unlikely to be able to argue for such an outcome, given all the other factors involved in heart disease. A weaker conclusion would be that reducing fat in our diet reduces the risk of heart disease. B and C are more general, weaker conclusions.

ACTIVITY 46

Below are some possible arguments.

A
R Studying at A Level is very different from GCSE.
R Sixth-form students are given more independence than other pupils.
IC Therefore sixth-form students are treated differently from other pupils.
R If sixth-form students don't have better facilities in school, they may leave to go to a college.
C Therefore, sixth-form students should have better facilities in school.

B
R Fish feel pain from the hook.
R Fish suffer when out of the water.
IC Fishing results in distress to the fish.
R There is no purpose in the activity, as the fish are not eaten once caught.
C We should consider banning the sport of fishing.

C
R Traffic speeds are far higher on motorways than on normal roads.

R   Motorways have three lanes of traffic, unlike all other types of road.
IC There are significant differences between motorways and other roads.
R   Newly qualified drivers only have experience of these other types of road.
C   Therefore newly qualified drivers should not be allowed to drive on motorways.

All of the above arguments could be improved by including unstated assumptions as an extra reason.

ACTIVITY 47

Below are two possible answers for arguments A and C.

A
R   Studying at A Level is very different to GCSE.
E.g. Sudents are expected to do background reading.
R   Sixth-form students are given more independence than other pupils.
E.g. Sixth-form students have study periods where they are expected to organise their own learning.
IC Therefore, sixth-form students are treated differently from other pupils.
R   If sixth-form students don't have better facilities in school, they may leave to go to a college.
Ev The college in town has a common room with pool table and television, and 10% of last year's Year 11 left to go there.
C   Therefore, sixth-form students should have better facilities in school.

C
R   Traffic speeds are far higher on motorways than on normal roads.
Ev The speed limit is 70mph.
R   Motorways have three lanes of traffic, unlike all other types of road.
IC There are significant differences between motorways and other roads.
R   Newly qualified drivers only have experience of these other types of road.
Ex Such as single carriageway A roads.
C   Therefore, newly qualified drivers should not be allowed to drive on motorways.

ACTIVITY 48

Below are two possible answers.

A
CA Although many people who are not Christian celebrate Christmas ...
R   Christmas is one of the two most important Christian festivals.
R   The UK is still considered to be a Christian country.
Ev The Queen is head of the Church of England.
IC It would be wrong to lose the Christian meaning of the festival in the UK.
R   For Christians the focus of Christmas is the birth of Jesus, even if other people are more concerned with presents and having lots of parties.
C   Therefore Christmas should not be renamed Winterfest.

B
CA Although Pilates and Yoga are good forms of exercise.
R   Sportsmen and women need specific forms of exercise to improve their performance.
Ex Rugby players need to do regular weight training to improve their muscle strength.
R   Other sports require that you spend time practising that sport.
E.g. You can only get better at horse riding by spending many hours riding.
IC Some sports need types of training not covered by Yoga and Pilates.

R   Many people find it hard to concentrate during these exercises.
C   It is not necessarily the case that everyone would benefit from Pilates and Yoga.

As most of these activities involve students developing their own arguments, there are no right or suggested answers – just many different lines of reasoning and better or worse ways of structuring that reasoning. Students can be helped by using the mark schemes to mark their arguments.

Suggestions have been made for four activities to aid thought processes. These are not intended to be exhaustive.

ACTIVITY 52

This activity is intended to get students thinking about the different sorts of special needs and the different sorts of responses to those needs. Assumptions include:

Assumption: children in wheelchairs (i.e. children with physical disabilities) are also intellectually impaired.
Challenge: A child who needs a wheelchair because of paralysed legs may well be extremely bright and very well able to cope with the intellectual demands of a mainstream school.

Assumption: Mainstream schools have no responsibility to change to make education accessible to those with special needs.
Challenge: Mainstream schools do have a moral (and legal?) responsibility to make classrooms and facilities accessible to those with physical disabilities, e.g. by including ramps and lifts in school buildings.

ACTIVITY 56

a) Principles that may be used include, but are not limited to: I have a duty to pay a price for goods that allows the producer a living wage; we should not exploit others; we should help those less fortunate than ourselves.

b) Principles that may be used include, but are not limited to: I have a duty to protect my family from misfortune/we should provide for times of hardship; we should all take responsibility for our finances.

ACTIVITY 57

a) Crossing the road. Although this seems to be an area in which the government should leave us to our own devices, the government does restrict how and when we can cross the road to a certain extent; at zebra and pedestrian crossings pedestrians have right of way over cars (if the green man is visible). At junctions, pedestrians have right of way over cars turning into a side road if they are already in the road. At other times, cars and other vehicles legally have the right of way. Jaywalkers – people who just walk out into the road – can be prosecuted, as well as injured. The law (which is the instrument of governments) would not support a person who walked in front of a car without looking. This is actually a good thing, as otherwise there would be chaos.

b) Support: People should be protected from their own excesses; governments have a duty to create order; governments have a duty to promote a healthy, safe lifestyle. Challenge: The government should restrict its activities to the economy and defence; governments should not affect our personal lives; individuals should be able to exercise freedom of choice in personal matters.

ACTIVITY 58

a) We should treat people with the politeness and consideration we would like to be treated with – for example, we should hold the door for someone struggling with lots of bags, as we would hope that others would hold the door for us in similar circumstances.

We should remain calm when driving rather than shouting at the idiots around us.

We should not deceive or be rude about our friends. We would like them to be honest with us and polite about us.

b) Support: Everyone should be treated equally; we should treat people as an end in themselves and not as a means to our own ends; it would be unfair to expect special treatment for ourselves.

Challenge: People should be treated as they wish to be treated (not as I would wish to be treated); people should be treated as they deserve to be treated (criminals, liars, etc.).

Unit 2 Section A: Sample answers

Guidance to the multiple-choice questions

1. d)

   a) Neither of these sentences gives us a reason to accept the other, so it cannot be an argument. An argument must have a reason and a conclusion.

   b) This explains how stem cell research can help scientists. It is not trying to persuade us to accept a conclusion.

   c) This is information about scientists who have studied molecular biology. It is not trying to persuade us of anything.

   d)

   R Some techniques involve creating embryos and removing stem cells.
   R This kills the embryo.
   R It seems wrong to create life in order to kill it.
   C Using stem cells from embryos for research is morally worrying.

2. b) This passage offers the opinion that satire is as necessary in the twenty-first century as it was in the mid-twentieth century. It offers no support for this claim, but provides a list of examples of comedy and satire.

   Is this:

   a) The examples do not explain anything. They simply list a number of comedy shows.

   c) There are no logical links of support in this passage. None of the claims or examples gives us any reason to accept any of the others.

   d) The sentences are not unconnected because they are all about comedy and satire. The examples are related to the opinion about satire being necessary.

Unit 2 Guidance to the Activities

OCR AS Critical Thinking

3. b) See analysis that follows.

CA		
	R	People believe that chemicals are bad additives.
	C (of CA)	Some may argue that it (claiming not to use chemicals) is a sensible advertising ploy,
	R	However, food is made of chemicals.
	Ex	Water is a chemical.
	Ex	Lemon juice is mostly the chemical citric acid.
	C	Food companies that claim that they do not use chemicals in their products are talking complete nonsense.

    a) Conclusion of counter-argument.

    c) Reason and two examples.

    d) Reason in counter-argument.

4. c) This is a principle, a general claim that would act as a guide to action. It weakens the argument by showing that striking can be justified if people are fighting for what is right.

    a) This claim would weaken the argument but it is a statement of fact not a principle.

    b) This is not a principle, although it would slightly weaken the argument.

    d) This is a principle but it would strengthen the argument.

Guidance for Questions 5, 6 and 7

Analysis

Counter-argument

R (of CA)	Children living with single parents are more likely to experience serious illness than those living with married parents.
C (of CA)	The tax and benefit system should be changed to encourage couples to stay together
R	The proportion of families headed by a lone parent has barely changed over the past ten years.
IC	So there is no evidence that the existing tax and benefit system is encouraging people to live apart.
R	Furthermore, most lone parents have been married, and their average age is 36.
Ev	Nearly 60% are in paid work.
C	However, tweaking the tax and benefit system is unlikely to affect the number of lone parent families.

5. a) See analysis.

    b) This is only the conclusion of the counter-argument, not the whole counter-argument.

    c) This is not a counter-assertion, because it is supported by a reason. This makes it the conclusion of the counter-argument.

    d) This is the conclusion of the counter-argument.

6. b) See analysis.

    a) This is not evidence as it is not facts, figures or information. It is supported by a reason and gives further support to the main conclusion, so it is an intermediate conclusion.

c) This cannot be the main conclusion of the argument because it gives further support to the claim that tweaking the tax and benefit system is unlikely to affect the number of lone parent families. This makes it an intermediate conclusion.

d) This is supported by the reason 'the proportion of families headed by a lone parent has barely changed over the past ten years'. So it cannot be a reason. As it also gives support to the main conclusion, it is an intermediate conclusion.

7. d) Tax and benefits were very different in the nineteenth century than they are today. The Welfare state which provides benefits was only introduced in the middle of the twentieth century. So, if there were a similar number of families headed by lone parent families when there was no welfare state and therefore no benefits, the conclusion that 'tweaking' tax and benefits will not affect the number of lone parent families is considerably strengthened.

a) This does have relevance to the argument because it allows us to compare the number of lone parent families now with the number at a time when there were no benefits.

b) This does strengthen the argument.

c) This strengthens the argument.

Guidance for Questions 8 and 9

Analysis

CA Although the Festival of Halloween has a long history, dating back to Celtic Druids,
R1 First of all, it encourages superstition in a modern, scientific world,
R2 which cannot be a good thing.
R3 Second, it is commercial theft, an occasion hyped up to take our money from us.
R4 Also not a good thing.
R5 We must either encourage children to beg with menaces or cower in our darkened homes all evening.
IC It glorifies criminal behaviour.
R6 This is unacceptable.
C   We should fight against it in a modern world.

8. b) See analysis.

   a) This combines Rs 2, 4 and 6.

   c) Counter-assertion.

   d) This combines R5 and R6.

9. c) R5 claims that we must 'either encourage children to beg with menaces or cower in our darkened homes all evening'. This clearly restricts the options to two extremes and ignores the middle ground of carrying on normally, or engaging in Trick or treating with small children as a fun activity.

   a) There is no conflation. The author has restricted the options to either encourage children to beg with menaces or cower in our darkened homes all evening.

   b) The author does not confuse cause and effect. The author has restricted the options to either encourage children to beg with menaces or cower in our darkened homes all evening.

   d) There is no slippery slope. There is some exaggeration, but there is not a sequence of logically unconnected and increasingly extreme links.

Unit 2 Guidance to the Activities OCR AS Critical Thinking

10.
- a) The argument moves from evidence about Pacific crows using tools to the conclusion that birds are clearly much more intelligent than we previously believed. This is a hasty generalisation from specific to general on the basis of too little evidence.
- b) The argument does not conclude that crows in general make tools. It does make a generalisation, but it generalises from the crows that were filmed to birds in general.
- c) The author does not imply a cause and effect relationship. This answer is expressing a flaw that the author has not made to distract you. Watch out for this!
- d) The argument does not assume that the crows knew that they were making tools.

Guidance for Questions 11 and 12

Context: For a long time science has held that humans were the only mammal females which do not show signs of coming into heat, or 'oestrus' when they are at their most fertile.

Ev Research indicates that women put more effort into their appearance when they are fertile,
Ex choosing more revealing tops and more seductive perfumes.
Ev New studies show that lap dancers earn bigger tips when they are in the fertile part of their cycle.
C   There are signs when women are fertile.

11. d)
- a) Context – background information to set up the rest of the argument.
- b) This is evidence to support the conclusion.
- c) This is evidence to support the conclusion.

12. c) Heightened desire and thoughts of babies at the most fertile time of the month would count as signs that a woman was fertile.
- a) This claim might weaken the argument at least partly, by showing that any signs that women are fertile are very subtle and can easily be missed.
- b) Becoming bad tempered and snappy just before a period would indicate that there are signs that a woman is not fertile. This would not strengthen the specific conclusion that there are signs when a woman is fertile.
- d) Changes in body odour, etc., would indicate that a woman is not fertile at a particular time. This would not strengthen the specific conclusion that there are signs when a woman is fertile.

13. d) We can see from the graph that there are many more women in their 70s and 80s than men. Figures for other ages are roughly the same. So we can conclude that this difference is because women are living longer than men.
- a) Figures for most age groups are similar, so we cannot conclude that more boys are born than girls. We also do not know how these figures are affected by immigration and emigration.
- b) There is no information given about the proportions of immigrants or emigrants or people who are born in the UK and live their whole lives in the same country. The higher numbers of people in their late thirties to late forties could be accounted for by a baby

boom in the 1960s, or by an influx of immigrants in their late teens and early twenties during the 1990s. So we cannot conclude that most immigrants are between 37–48 years old.

c) We cannot conclude that the birth rate increased during this period because the graph shows that there are fewer 3–7-year-olds than either 10-year-olds or very small babies. It seems to indicate that the birth rate decreased from 1995–2000, and then increased from 2000–2005.

Guidance for Questions 14 and 15

Analysis

R   If we all lived healthy lives for two hundred or more years, there would be a population explosion which the planet could not sustain.

IC   We might have to face moral questions about which elderly people to terminate to make way for the young.

R   If the population were vastly too large, we might have to consider whether some genetically inferior young people should be sterilised.

R   These dilemmas would be unbearably difficult.

IC   It is much easier for nature to make these decisions for us.

C   We should rejoice in the beers, burgers and bonking which make it likely that we will all die naturally within a normal life span.

14. b) See analysis.

    a) This is a paraphrase of an intermediate conclusion.

    c) This is a conclusion that could be drawn from the reasoning.

    d) This is not a part of the argument.

15. b) The argument shows that it would be best for the species to have a population that dies fairly young (i.e. not at 200) because the planet cannot sustain too many people. It uses this to support the conclusion that we should be glad about the bad habits that ensure we die fairly young. However, although it may be best for the species if we eat unhealthily etc., it is not best for each individual. From an individual point of view, we cannot be glad about bad habits which mean we will die young. So the argument has ignored important considerations.

    a) This tries to distract you by making you think that the author has confused necessary and sufficient conditions. This is not what the author has done, though.

    c) This is a tricky distractor. The argument does use hypothetical reasoning, but the consequences are not implausible. If people did live to 200, we would have to consider euthanasia and controls on breeding. We are already considering euthanasia, and some countries put limits on the number of babies people can have. There have in the past been programmes to sterilise people who were thought to be inferior to stop them having children.

    d) This answer tries to distract you by making you think that there might be a slippery slope flaw in the argument. However, although there are problems with the logic, the argument is not a slippery slope. It is the starting point which is extreme, not the conclusion.

Unit 2 Sections B and C: Sample answers

Guidance to Analysing and evaluating argument

1. We should support the EU directive to ban the sale of a wide range of health supplements.

2. The EU directive is an infringement to the right to freedom of choice

3.
   - The author is generalising from the one example of Vitamin C (a vitamin) to all health supplements, which includes minerals and plant extracts, so this does not support the reasoning that health supplements do a lot of damage to people's health
   - A dose of 5000 milligrams is very high and is not representative of a typical dose that someone might take so this does not support the author's reason that health supplements do a lot of damage to people's health

4. a) *Ad hominen* or attacking the arguer.

4. b) Rather than engaging with the argument and explaining why the research that shows Vitamin C supplements help prevent heart disease, the author simply dismisses the opposing view by attacking the spokesman from the Health Supplements Industry for being biased. But this bias does not necessarily mean that the view is incorrect. The research could have come from an independent source.

5. a) This evidence is not relevant. It is about pills replacing food whereas the passage is about pills which people take to supplement their diet / It is not really evidence – it is an anecdote about the opinions/predictions of science fiction writers (*not* scientists) so it is unreasonable to use it as evidence about what might really happen.

5. b)
   - Eating meals is about more than just getting fuel for our bodies; people enjoy the social side of sitting down and eating together
   - Although busy, people enjoy preparing and cooking food.
   - Many people now own microwaves which makes cooking food a lot quicker
   - People like eating!

6. a) Restricting the Options (also known as False Dichotomy or Either/Or flaw)

6. b) The author's reasoning is flawed as he implies that there are only two options, people either take pills or they lead a healthy lifestyle. Many people take health supplements as part of a healthy lifestyle to ensure their bodies receive the right balance of vitamins and minerals. So this reasoning does not show that people take too many pills, or that we should therefore support the EU directive.

7. This evidence is not relevant. Painkillers alleviate the effects of ill-health whereas food supplements aim to prevent ill health in the first place, so this does not support the idea that people already take too many pills instead of adopting a healthier lifestyle.

8. a) Being forced to wear seat belts in cars is being compared to not being allowed to buy health supplements. Not opposing the EU directive is being compared to not opposing the law about seatbelts. Just as no one opposed the law on wearing seatbelts we shouldn't oppose the EU directive on banning health supplements.

8. b) Both pieces of legislation are about seeking to prevent people being harmed.

8. c) Being made to wear a seatbelt in a car involves the wellbeing of others (passengers) whereas taking health supplements, or being prevented from taking them, is just about the well being of the individual. Not wearing a seatbelt is irresponsible because crashes do huge damage to people not wearing seatbelts so it seems reasonable for the government to make us wear seatbelts. Dietary supplements are an attempt made by people to look after themselves, so government interference seems less reasonable.

9. Paragraph 6 states that we cannot get too much vitamins and minerals yet paragraph 2 includes research that too high a dose of Vitamin C could lead to cancer.

Total [28]

Guidance to Developing your own arguments

10. Just because people are no longer able to buy health supplements does not necessarily mean that they will buy more fruit and vegetables.

    - Some people use health supplements because they are too busy and/or lazy to cook and prepare food, so they take a dose of multivitamins rather than spend time checking that their diet contains the required amount of vitamins such as Vitamin C and minerals such as iron.
    - The cost of health supplements might be cheaper than the cost of the amount of fruit and vegetables needed to be bought to get the equivalent dose of vitamins and/or minerals, for example the cost of the amount of spinach you would need to eat to get the recommended daily dose of iron could be more than the cost of an iron tablet.

11. A possible argument challenging the principle that would access the top band of marks:

    CA Some people might argue that the government should pass legislation preventing us from harming ourselves as this can lead to an unnecessary drain on the National Health Service and the Emergency Services
    Eg for example when people need to be air-lifted to hospital after rock climbing accidents.
    CA You might even want to argue that it is appropriate for the government to pass laws to preventing us from harming other people
    Eg 30 miles speed restriction in residential areas has led to a success reduction in the number of children killed in road traffic accidents.
    R1 However, once a person is over the age of eighteen they should be mature enough to make their own decisions and take responsibility for their own actions
    R2 The government has a duty to inform its citizens of the risks involved with activities that may be harmful
    Eg as is the case with the warning on cigarette packets, but we should be free to decide for ourselves
    R3 If the government prevented us from doing things that were harmful, this would mean that many (Hyp R) activities that people enjoy might become illegal.
    Eg For example, many people derive an immense amount of pleasure from horse riding as well as it being a good way of keeping fit
    IC We would miss out on the many benefits of activities that might be considered harmful
    C Governments should not pass laws to prevent us from harming ourselves.

12. An example of an argument against the conclusion which would access the top band of marks:

    CA There are concerns about the widespread use of Health supplements
    IC however, there are both psychological and health benefits from taking health supplements.

R1 It is suggested that these supplements act as a placebo. People feel better from taking them, even though they are having no effect on the actual condition.

Ev A study for Loughborough University has shown that many people claim improvements to joint pain after taking Glucosamine Sulphate even though there is no medical research showing that these tablets reduce inflammation in joints.

Eg Similarly many people take Echinacea early in the winter believing it will reduce their chances of catching colds and flu.

R2 Health supplements are also a good thing as they enable people who are too busy to eat properly to obtain the vitamins and minerals they need for a balanced diet.

Eg A daily Multivitamin tablet means that you don't have to remember to eat at least 5 portions of fruit and vegetables

R3 A decline in sales of health supplements could have a negative effect on the health supplement industry. This could leading to redundancies.

MC We should not support the EU directive to ban the sale of a wide range of health supplements.

Total [28]

Total Sections B and C [56]

AS Critical Thinking CD-ROMs

Opposite you will find three AS Critical Thinking CD-ROMs:

Student VLE CD-ROM

This is a version of the CD-ROM located in the back of the Student Book.
It is designed to run on a VLE. This CD-ROM comprises:

 **LiveText**

On the CD-ROM you will find an electronic version of the Student Book, powered by LiveText.
As well as the Student Book and the LiveText tools there is also:

- **G** guidance to the activities – indicated by this icon

- Interactive activities to help develop your students' Critical Thinking skills further – indicated by this icon.

Within the electronic version of the Student Book, you will also find the interactive Exam Café.

 **Exam Café**

Here students can immerse themselves in our contemporary interactive Exam Café environment! With a click of your mouse they can visit three separate areas in the café to **Relax, Refresh your Memory** or **Get the Result**.
They will find a wealth of material including:
- Revision Tips from students, Key Concepts, Common Mistakes and Examiner's Tips
- Language of the Exam (an interactive activity)
- Revision Flashcards, Revision Checklists and The Basics
- Sample Exam Questions (which they can try) with student answers and examiner comments.

Planning and Delivery Resource File standalone CD-ROM

This is a version of the CD-ROM located in the back of the Student Book. It is a standalone CD-ROM and comprises all the content listed for the Student VLE CD-ROM above plus:

Planning and Delivery Resource File

Embedded at the beginning of each chapter of the electronic Student Book you will find editable files of the Planning and Delivery File.

Planning and Delivery Resource File VLE CD-ROM

This is a version of the Planning and Delivery Resource File standalone CD-ROM designed to run on a VLE.
It comprises all the same content listed above, including the embedded editable files from the Planning and Delivery File.

Minimum system requirements for all three CD-ROMs:

- Windows 2000, XP Pro or Vista
- Internet Explorer 6 (and above) or Firefox 2.0
- Flash Player 8 or higher plug-in
- Pentium III 1GHz Intel® with 512Mb RAM
- Screen Resolution: 800 x 600 or higher

VLE
SCORM 1.2-compliant web-based VLE,
e.g. Kaleidos v3, Moodle, Fronter

Product installation

Run the software direct from the CD

To run your CD, insert it into the CD drive of your computer.
It should start automatically; if not, please go to My Computer (Computer on Vista), double-click on the 'package' folder, then click **LiveText.exe** and run software from there.

Installation on a VLE
Separate disks are supplied for installation on a VLE. Insert the VLE Pack CD-ROM in a network CD-ROM drive.
Use your VLE's own 'import' feature and browse to the CD-ROM.

If you have difficulties running the CD, or if your copy is not there, please contact the helpdesk number given below.

Software support
For further software support between the hours of 8.30–5.00
(Mon–Fri), please contact:
Tel: 01865 888108
Fax: 01865 314091
Email: software.enquiries@pearson.com